The Bible
on the
Life Hereafter

The Bible
on the
Life Hereafter

William Hendriksen

BakerBooks

A Division of Baker Book House Co
Grand Rapids, Michigan 49516

© 1959 by William Hendriksen

Published by Baker Books
a division of Baker Book House Company
P.O. Box 6287, Grand Rapids, MI 49516-6287

Trade paperback edition
Eighth printing 1995

Printed in the United States of America

ISBN 0-8010-4022-1

Preface

The life hereafter is a subject of universal and timeless interest. This is as it should be. Man is created for eternity. This present life, however significant, is only the beginning of a never ending life of weal or woe.

The Bible has much to say on the latter days and the life hereafter. Much of this is for our warning and admonition. However, even more is to help us to live a God-honoring life on earth in joyful anticipation of a God-glorifying life of bliss in heaven. Those who fail to study what the Bible says about the future life miss much of comfort and joy.

There is widespread difference of opinion on the life hereafter. This is in the main due to two reasons. Sinful man is reluctant to face the facts presented by Scripture. Man is inclined to reason and speculate beyond the data furnished in God's Word. The author of this book seeks to remain true to Scripture throughout.

This book is for anyone desirous of knowing God's plan for man's life. It is constructed in such a way that it can as readily be used for group study and discussion as for personal reference. It is a major contribution to the literature on the future life.

The publisher is happy to make this book available to the reading public.

THE PUBLISHER

Table of Contents

INTRODUCTION

INDIVIDUAL ESCHATOLOGY
Part I. Death and Immortality

Part II. The Intermediate State

GENERAL ESCHATOLOGY
Part I. The Signs

Part II. The Second Coming

Part III.
Events Associated with the Second Coming

Part IV. The Final State

Introduction

Chapter 1

Are You Living in Three Tenses?

Read Psalm 116:1-9; 73:23-25

1. The Christian Life Is a Life in Three Tenses

The author of Psalm 116 was reliving *the past*. He had been in peril of losing his life. He says:

> "*The cords of death compassed me,*
> *And the pangs of Sheol laid hold on me:*
> *I found trouble and sorrow.*"

But in the midst of his distress and anguish he had called on the name of Jehovah. Out of the depths he had uttered the cry for help: "O Jehovah, I beseech thee, deliver my soul." And Jehovah had heard him, and this in such a wonderful manner that, in addition to delivering his soul from death, he had also delivered his eyes from tears and even his feet from falling. Hence, with a view to *the past, gratitude* filled the poet's heart, causing him to exclaim, "I love Jehovah." Yes, the poet is exercising his faith with reference to *the past*.

The marvelous fact is, however, that it is not possible for the believer, *if he be consistent,* to live solely in the past. Spiritually he necessarily lives *in three tenses;* hence also in the present and in the future. Why is this true? Offhand we would say that it might be possible for him to think, "Yes, Jehovah was wonderful to me in the past; but as to the present I am not so sure, and as to the future, I am very uncertain." The reason why the believer who reasons consistently cannot argue in that fashion is this: he knows that Jehovah is *unchangeable.* Does not his very name *Jehovah* imply this? Hence, he who was the believer's *help* in the past, is his *strength* in the present, and his *hope* for the future. The author of Psalm 116 understood this. Most beautifully he is living in all three tenses — *the past:* "Thou *hast*

15

delivered my soul from death," etc.; *the present:* "Gracious *is* Jehovah and righteous. Yea, our God *is* merciful"; *the future:* "Therefore *will I call* upon him *as long as I live.*"

And if you will now turn to Psalm 73, you will immediately notice that Asaph, with the reasoning of a God-given faith, draws the same inference. He, too, was able to tell about an amazing experience he had lived through. As he looks back upon a stretch of the path that lies behind him, he is willing to confess that he had come very near to tripping and to falling headlong. "I almost slipped," you hear him say. "I nearly lost my footing." Why? Because of the perplexing manner in which God's providence was operating. Instead of the righteous prospering and the wicked being afflicted, the exact opposite was happening again and again. In his bewilderment Asaph had been tempted to say, "It just is not fair, the way God is running this world." But then in God's sanctuary it had been called to his attention that this present life can never be properly evaluated unless it be seen in the light of the eternity that awaits the children of men. A very sharp contrast had been drawn between *the end* of the wicked and *the end* of the righteous. He saw it all now. And the result? He, too, exercises his faith. Yes, he exercises it *in three tenses.* As to *the present:* "I am continually with thee." As to *the past:* "*Thou hast taken* hold of my right hand." And as to *the future:* "*Thou wilt guide* me with thy counsel, And *afterward* receive me to glory."

2. The Christian Life, Accordingly, Includes the Future

Did you ever notice that Paul, too, most beautifully lives in the past ("It is Christ Jesus *who died,* yea rather, *who was raised* from the dead"); the present ("*who is* at the right hand of God, *who also makes intercession* for us"); and the future ("*Who shall separate us* from the love of Christ?"). Not only "things present" but also "things to come" belong even now to us (Romans 8:38; I Corinthians 3:23).

The believer, then, *is grateful* as to the past, *restful* as to the present, and *trustful* as to the future.

That *trustfulness* as to the future will engage our attention in this book.

FOR DISCUSSION

A. *Based on This Chapter*

1. Show that the author of Psalm 116 was exercising his faith with respect to the past, the present, and the future.

2. Show that the author of Psalm 73 was doing the same.

3. Just why is it that, having experienced God's goodness in the past, we immediately infer that this same goodness is being exercised toward us in the present, and that it will also be shown to us in the future?

4. Prove from Scripture that Paul also lived "in three tenses."

5. Which of the three is the theme of this book?

B. *Further Discussion*

1. Is it possible for a mere animal — a dog or a monkey — to meditate upon his future? Is it possible for the average adult person *never* to meditate upon his future? In the light of your answer to these questions, what inference can you draw with respect to the theory of evolution?

2. Is there a danger that a person should begin to pay too much attention to his future state, thereby neglecting his present duty? How can this danger be avoided?

3. Is there also the opposite danger, namely, that a person should begin to lay too much stress on past experiences and present circumstances, thereby neglecting his hope for eternity? How can this danger be avoided?

4. Can you mention any sects which, as you see it, entertain "queer" beliefs concerning the future?

5. What is the best way to guard ourselves against being won over by these sects?

Chapter 2

What Is Eschatology? How Is It Divided?

Read Psalm 90:10-12; I Thessalonians 5:1-11

1. "Eschatology" — What Is Meant by It?

We turn then to the future. The systematic study of that which the Bible has revealed to us in regard to our individual future and the future of the world and of mankind in general is called *Eschatology*. It has been called "the crown and capstone of theology." Apart from it the doctrine of God, man, Christ, salvation, the church, remains incomplete. It is the doctrine of *the consummation*.

The term *Eschatology* comes from two Greek words: *eschatos* and *logos*. *Eschatos* means *last*, and *logos* means *word* or *discourse*. *Eschatology* is therefore *a discourse about the last things*. It has to do with those things that are going to happen last of all; that is, at the close of man's earthly life and afterward, and also toward the close of the present dispensation and afterward.

2. Moses and Paul Speak in Terms of Eschatology

A careful reading of Psalm 90 shows that Moses was speaking in eschatological terms. And a perusal of I Thessalonians 5:1-11 will convince one that the apostle Paul did the same thing.

Nevertheless, between these two sections of Scripture there is a difference in approach. You will have noticed that Moses in Psalm 90 speaks about *the end of man's life as an individual*. He places over against one another God's eternity and man's transitoriness. God is "from everlasting to everlasting," but man's life may span seventy years or perhaps if he be very strong eighty years. "It is soon gone and we fly away." The lesson, of course, is this, "So teach us to number our days, that we may get a heart of wisdom."

Paul, too, in I Thessalonians 5 is reflecting on *the end*, yet not mainly on the end of man's life as an individual but rather on *the end of the present dispensation*. Among the Thessalonians

18

there was curiosity concerning the exact time when Christ's second coming would take place. How long did God's children still have to wait? Just when was Jesus going to arrive? Basing his answer on previous teaching which had come straight from the mouth of the Lord, Paul states that the readers have no need of further information on this subject. If they will but reflect, they will recall that they have been repeatedly shown that, according to the word of the Lord (Matthew 24:43), the day of his return will be "like a thief in the night." He will come very suddenly, taking people by surprise. As to the wicked, the Lord will come upon them while they are saying, "Peace and safety." They will be *wholly unprepared.* Hence, sudden destruction will come upon them. In that respect believers are different. Moreover, they should endeavor to be different, for by God's grace they are filled with the light of salvation. Says Paul, "We belong neither to night nor to darkness," the night and the darkness of sin and unbelief. He continues, "Accordingly, let us not sleep as do the rest, but let us remain watchful and sober."

3. Eschatology, Accordingly, Is Divided into Two Branches: Individual and General Eschatology

As we have now seen, Moses in Psalm 90 speaks in terms of *Individual Eschatology.* Paul in I Thessalonians 5, although not entirely omitting this phase of the subject, is mainly dealing with *General Eschatology.*

Although it makes little difference which is discussed first, so that one could discuss *General Eschatology* before *Individual Eschatology,* yet a good reason can be given for treating *Individual Eschatology* first. After all, during the course of history, death for the individual *precedes* Christ's second coming. By means of death, moreover, the individual is transferred into the age to come. As to time, death is very clearly an *individual* matter. Now *one* dies, then *another.* The name *Individual Eschatology* is given to whatever Scripture reveals concerning the condition of the individual between his death and the general resurrection at the close of the age.

That such a study is necessary will be readily seen. There is much confusion on this subject. Some believe that when a person dies he simply ceases to be. He goes "out of existence." Another believes that the souls of most believers go to purgatory. Still another is of the opinion that we cannot know anything about such matters, or that for both the believer and the unbeliever death means a lapsing into a state of unconsciousness which lasts until the day of the resurrection. It is therefore very necessary for us to examine what the Bible itself says with respect to *Individual Eschatology*.

But it is equally necessary to study *General Eschatology*. It is easy to see why this second division is called *General Eschatology*. It has reference to men *in general*. People die individually and separately, now one, then another. But they will arise *together* and will be judged *together*. When our Lord returns, *every eye* will see him. "The great and the small" will stand before the throne. As to both soul and body the wicked will then be assigned to hell *together*, and the righteous to the renewed heaven and earth *together*.

Also with respect to this subject of *General Eschatology* there is disbelief and confusion. Many people are of the opinion that things will simply continue as they are now. They refuse to believe that history is moving onward toward a mighty crisis. And even in the minds of those who *do* believe in a coming crisis there are many notions that are not at all Scriptural.

Accordingly, it is our purpose in this book, after an Introductory Section, upon which we have already entered, to discuss *Individual Eschatology* and then *General Eschatology*.

FOR DISCUSSION

A. *Based on This Chapter*

1. What is meant by Eschatology?
2. About what does Moses speak in Psalm 90?
3. About what does Paul speak in I Thessalonians 5?
4. Into what two branches, accordingly, is Eschatology divided?
5. Why is it necessary to study both Individual and General Eschatology?
6. What good reason is there to study Individual Eschatology before General Eschatology?

B. *Further Discussion*

1. Are there any Scripture-passages which show that a truly converted man is deeply interested in the subject of Eschatology?

2. Is there any relation between deep interest in this subject and sanctified living?

3. Are differences of opinion on subjects such as these wholesome or dangerous?

4. What sections of the Bible deal particularly with Eschatology?

5. Do ministers preach too many sermons on such subjects or too few? Give reasons for your opinion.

Chapter 3

But Is This Study Practical?

Read I Peter 3:8-16; 4:7-11; 5:8, 9

There are those who maintain that the study of the doctrine of the last things takes us too far away from our duty in the here and now. But this need not be true. In fact, if these truths are seen in their proper, Biblical contexts they become a mighty power for good in this present life.

The apostle Peter, in the section read, was thinking about "the end of all things" (I Peter 4:7). This did not in any way cause him to lose contact with present duty. On the contrary, it served as an incentive to arouse in his own heart and in the hearts and minds of the readers a sense of urgency in the fulfilment of present spiritual tasks.

The practical significance of Scripture's doctrine concerning the future may be summarized as follows:

1. *The teaching concerning the blessing to be inherited (here and in the hereafter) encourages men so to live that this reward will be theirs (read I Peter 3:8, 9).* It is entirely proper for the believer to seek a reward (Matthew 19:29; cf. Hebrews 12:1, 2), provided that it be his purpose to use that reward to the glory of God (in the spirit of Revelation 4:10, 11).

2. *The teaching with respect to heaven's reward and hell's punishment furnishes a stimulus and a theme for Christian mission work (read I Peter 3:10-12).* Cf. Psalm 2:12; Matthew 10:28; Acts 2:40; 17:30, 31; Romans 5:9; II Corinthians 5:20, 21; and Revelation 21:7).

3. *The study and practice of these Biblical truths helps one to answer enquirers and to put to shame revilers (read I Peter 3:15, 16).*

4. *Meditation upon these things stimulates prayer (read I Peter 4:7).* Without prayer it will be impossible to be "of a sound

mind," ever ready to meet the adversary. Without prayer it will also be impossible to live the sanctified life or to carry on the great work of missions so that others may be rescued from the power of Satan and may inherit that everlasting bliss in which they will glorify and enjoy God forever.

5. *Reflection upon these truths strengthens love for one another (read I Peter 4:8-10).* Is it too strong a statement to make that those, and those *only,* who love the fellowship *here* (see Psalm 133) will partake of the fellowship *there?* See also Genesis 25:8; Matthew 8:11; Hebrews 12:1, 23.

6. *By means of earnest consideration of these matters and by living a life that results from such consideration God is glorified (read I Peter 4:11).* The *goodness* of God leads men to repentance (Romans 2:4). Contemplation of the wonderful things which God has in store for his children inspires gratitude and adoration. Thus God is glorified.

7. *The inner conviction that hell is real and that it is Satan's sinister purpose to devour as many people as possible is an incentive to steadfastness in the faith (read I Peter 5:8, 9).* We see, therefore, that, far from being impractical, these truths are of inestimable value for our present life. To neglect them would be a great error. Surely, every person who has his hope set on him who one day will be manifested in glory "purifies himself even as he is pure" (I John 3:3).

FOR DISCUSSION

A. *Based on This Chapter*

1. What objection is sometimes advanced against the study of the doctrine of the last things?

2. In general, how would you answer that objection?

3. What is the relation between the study of Eschatology and the work of Christian Missions?

4. What is the relation between the study of the doctrine of the last things and prayer?

5. Mention some other arguments which show that such a study is of real value for life in the here and now.

B. *Further Discussion*

1. The apostle Paul surely busied himself with the doctrine of the

last things. See, for example, his epistles to the Thessalonians. Prove from these epistles that they have great value for practical life from day to day.

2. What is the basic error of those whose heated arguments about the future seem to exert no wholesome influence upon daily living?

3. Is fear of hell, standing alone and by itself, a sufficient incentive to really consecrated living?

4. How would you deal with earnest individuals who are disturbed because they believe that fear of hell or of the coming judgment is the real and only reason for their religious practices?

5. Dr. H. Bavinck states, "Grace and salvation are the objects of God's delight; but God does not delight in sin, neither has he pleasure in punishment" (see H. Bavinck, *The Doctrine of God*, English translation, p. 390). Do you agree?

Chapter 4

In Our Reflections on the Life Hereafter, Must We Limit Ourselves to One Testament?

Read Micah 4:1-4; 5:2

1. A Mistake Often Made

In the Bible that is lying on my desk about one thousand pages are devoted to the Old Testament. The New Testament covers slightly less than three hundred pages. Nevertheless, it has become customary in certain circles to neglect almost completely the Old Testament in discussing the doctrine of the last things. When an explanation is demanded, the answer often given amounts to this, "The Old Testament says nothing about the future of the individual and almost nothing about the consummation of all things."

But this opinion about the Old Testament, as if its doctrine with respect to the last things was very vague, is an exaggeration. It should be readily granted that revelation progresses, and that we shall be able to gather more of our eschatological material from the New than from the Old Testament. But:

2. The Old Testament *Does* Have a Doctrine of the Future

It is clear from the passage that was read that the Old Testament, as well as the New, tells us what *is* going to happen, or at least what *was* going to happen. Note the words of Micah 4:1, "But in the latter days it shall come to pass."

We must guard against two erroneous extremes. *On the one hand,* there are people who ignore the Old Testament. That is too bad. It is impossible fully to understand the New Testament if one knows very little about the Old. Old and New Testament

belong together. In numerous passages the Old Testament predicts the future, *both with respect to individuals and* with respect
to nations, in fact *even with respect to the universe in general.*
See, for example, such passages as the following: Psalm 16:8-11;
17:15; 49:14, 15; 73:24; Job 14:14; 19:25-27; Hosea 6:2; 13:14;
Isaiah 25:6-8; 26:19; chapter 66; and think of all the Messianic
prohecies and the prophecies concerning Israel's Restoration.
Hence, we must never neglect the Old Testament.

3. Whenever We Study the Old Testament We Must Take the Old Testament Approach

We said a moment ago, "We must guard against *two* extremes."
One extreme has been pointed out, namely, the extreme of paying
no attention to the Old Testament, acting just as if it were not
there. There is, however, another extreme, which is also dangerous. It is the extreme of failing to consider Old Testament
passages from the Old Testament point of view or in the light
of the Old Testament historical background. The passage which
was read offers a good illustration. The passage states that the
mountain of Jehovah's house is going to be established on the
top of the mountains, and that it shall be exalted above the
hills, that peoples shall flow unto it, that out of Zion shall go
forth the law, and that there shall be wonderful, glorious peace,
so that every man shall sit under his vine and under his fig-
tree, etc.

When some people read this, they say, "Now is not this a clear
prediction of the coming millennium, in which Zion, that is,
the Jews, is going to be supreme, so that everybody will just
flow unto it, during this era of universal peace for one thousand
years *at the close of history?*"

But that is not a fair way to deal with the text. The only fair
way to deal with such passages is to imagine that you yourself
were living in the days of the prophet Micah, about seven
hundred years before Christ. The *primary* meaning of the
passage then is as follows: *There will come a time when Israel,
by means of the Christ born out of its midst, will be a spiritual
blessing to all the nations, and will impart abiding peace to all
those who embrace him by a living faith.* That this is the meaning is clear also from Micah 5:2, in which passage the birth of

Christ is announced. Read especially verse 5 of that chapter, "And this man shall be our peace." The Micah 4:1-4 passage has nothing to do with any millennium which, as many believe, will be set up by Christ when he returns.

Now I can imagine that at this point somebody will say, "But it says *In the latter days,* and so it must have reference to the end of the world." My answer is, Not *primarily.* The expression, "in the latter days" does not necessarily mean *the end of the world.* It simply means, "the days to come," the future. What is included in that future must be determined in each separate instance by the context. That it cannot in every instance refer exclusively or primarily to the days which immediately precede Christ's *second* coming is clear not only from our present passage but also from such a passage as Genesis 49:1. Jacob in blessing his sons was not thinking primarily of what would happen at the end of the world!

4. Other Characteristics of Old Testament Eschatology

a. *Prophetic Foreshortening*

The Old Testament often sees the future as you see two hills in the distance, far, far away. Let us imagine that the farthest one is a little higher than the nearest one, so that you can see them both. Now from such a great distance it may easily happen that you see both as if they were one hill, or at least as if the farthest one were situated right behind the nearest. But when you actually arrive at the first hill, you begin to notice that there is still a long distance to cover before you have reached that second one. Now read Malachi 3:1, 2, and see if you understand what I mean. The Old Testament prophet sees the first and the second coming of Christ as if they were one. The same thing applies to our present passage, Micah 4:1-4, as will become clear.

b. *Multiple Fulfilment*

Study again that beautiful passage treated in the present chapter, namely, Micah 4:1-4. Though in symbolical language it describes the conditions that were going to obtain with the first coming of Christ on earth, it is also clear, is it not, that this is not the complete and final fulfilment. The peace which

Christ brought at his first coming is, in turn, a symbol of that lasting and glorious peace which he will bring at his second coming, when in the most final sense "nation shall not lift up sword against nation, neither shall they learn war any more."

FOR DISCUSSION

A. *Based on This Chapter*

1. What is the mistake often made, and what are the two extremes against which one must guard in studying what the Old Testament has to say about the future?

2. What erroneous interpretation do some people give to the present passage, Micah 4:1-4?

3. What passage in chapter 5 proves that their interpretation is wrong?

4. What is the correct primary interpretation of the passage?

5. Name and explain two characteristics of Old Testament Eschatology, and show what light they shed on the meaning of Micah 4:1-4.

B. *Further Discussion*

1. We have emphasized that Old Testament prophecies must be studied in the light of the Old Testament background. But are we not thereby contradicting the rule that we must interpret Old Testament prophecies *in the light of the New Testament?*

2. There are those who say that everything in the Bible must be interpreted *literally.* What ridiculous picture do you get when you so interpret Matthew 5:13a, or Mark 12:40a?

3. In what chapter of Isaiah do you find this same prophecy?

4. What light do Luke 2:32 and II Peter 3:13 shed on the meaning of Micah 4:1-4?

5. Does the expression "in the last days" in Acts 2:17 refer to the end of the world?

Individual Eschatology

Chapter 5

Death. What Is Its Rate of Frequency? Its Basic Character? The Wrong and the Right Attitude Toward It?

Read Psalm 39:4-7; 23:4

1. How Frequent?

"Jehovah...let me know how frail I am...Surely every man is mere breath...He heaps up riches, and knows not who shall gather them." How very true are these words of Psalm 39! And you may add Psalm 90:10 and Psalm 103:15, 16. (Look them up.)

Take your watch and observe that second hand. Notice the seconds speed by. Here in the United States, last year, approximately *every twenty seconds a person died!* Think of it: three deaths every minute and that is leaving out of consideration those who died in their mother's womb. Incidentally, this does not mean that our country will soon be without inhabitants, for it should also be borne in mind that although <u>of late every *twenty* seconds there has been a death</u>, every *eight* seconds there has been a birth. This means that, at the present rate of birth, in a single year about as many babies are born in this country as was the entire population of the United States in the year 1790, that is, about four million.

But if even the annual death-rate *in our country* is shocking, what shall we say about the death-rate in *the world at large?* According to the most recent issue of *World Almanac,* the population of the United States is about 190 million, while the population of the entire world is almost 3 *billion.* That means that roughly the world's population is 16 times that of the United States. The death rate in most parts of the world is much higher than that in the United States. The death rate for the whole world would therefore be more than 16 times that in the United States or no less than one death every second!

2. What Is Its Basic Character?

What makes all this more terrifying is the fact that death in the human realm — yes, even *physical* death — is not a merely natural phenomenon. It is basically a punishment for sin, a divine "appointment" (Genesis 2:17; Hebrews 9:27). It is an element included in the curse which God pronounced on Adam and his posterity: "Dust thou art, and unto dust shalt thou return" (Genesis 3:19).

3. What Wrong Attitudes Should Be Avoided?

a. That of *the Christian Scientist*. His teaching is this: "Matter, sin, sickness, and death have no reality." But you cannot destroy death by denying its existence. Death laughs at Christian Science. The Christian Scientist should read Genesis 5:5, 8, 11, 14, 17, 20, 27, 31.

b. That of *the Escapist*. There are millions of them. They fear death, and so they scrupulously avoid all mention of it. It is said that Louis XV forbade his servants to mention the word *death* in his presence. The Chinese are afraid that by mentioning the word *death* they are inviting it! In our own Western society the word is also being avoided as much as possible. Other words and phrases are substituted, if the matter must be discussed at all. Death is a reality which natural man does not dare to face. But that attitude, too, cannot be the true solution. It can never give peace to the soul.

c. That of *the Fatalist or Stoic*. This person tries to make himself and others believe that he is not a bit afraid of death. Is not death, after all, natural? Then why not face it boldly? Why not approach it without any trepidation? "When I die, I rot," said someone. And perhaps he added, "What of it?" This, too, is no solution. This fellow is only whistling in the dark. He *acts* bravely; but remember, it's an act! Read Isaiah 57:21.

d. That of *the Blatant Infidel*. This man curses death. He defies it. Being at the point of death, with his last bit of strength he shakes his fist at the elements and falls back dead, or else dies gasping, "This is a dirty trick."

e. That of *the out-and-out Pessimist.* He is utterly tired of life, and finally puts himself to death. In the year 1956 more than 16,000 persons committed suicide in the United States alone. This, too, is no solution. See Genesis 9:6; I Corinthians 6:19. But see also Matthew 7:1.

f. That of *the Sentimentalist.* He gushes over death-bed scenes, grows very sentimental, and is convulsed with sobs when he reads the story of the death of little Nell, in Dickens' *Old Curiosity Shop.* He *enjoys* it, though!

g. That of *the Religious Fanatic with "martyr-complex."* Do not confuse this person with the *real* martyr, like Stephen. No, this individual actually seeks to be put to death, though he does not put himself to death. He believes, perhaps, that by offering himself to be put to death for the faith he can earn a martyr's crown and afterward be venerated on earth as a saint. The words of I Corinthians 13:3b might apply to him.

4. What Is the Christian Attitude?

By no means does *he* seek death. He knows very well that death is contrary to nature, and that it is his duty to wait until God relieves him from his earthly post. Yes, the believer knows that in and by itself death is shadow and not sunlight. It means separation of that which belongs together. But he also knows that it is not the Valley of Death which he will have to enter but only the Valley of the Shadow of Death (Psalm 23:4). Moreover, he is convinced that in that valley Jehovah will be with him. He is never alone. Nothing, not even death, can ever separate him from the love of God which is in Christ Jesus, his Lord.

Death, to be sure, is in its essence *separation. For the unbeliever* it indicates not only a separation of the body from the soul, and of the person from all that was dear to him on earth; it even means a separation from that manifestation of God's kindness of which even he, the unbeliever, was the object here in this life. *For the believer* the separation is not complete. In fact, the main element in this separation is entirely missing. God's kindness and love go with the believer to glory. There, too, he will meet friends again and riches, far better than here on earth. And at Christ's return the soul will be reunited with the body, the latter gloriously transformed.

All this is the result of the fact that death's curse was borne for the believer by Christ. And life's crown was merited for him by that same Lord. Hence, for the believer physical death has now become a cloud with a silver lining, and it is upon that silver lining that he rivets his main attention. And so he prepares himself for death. He looks unto Jesus, and from his heart there arises the triumphant cry: "Death is swallowed up in victory..." (I Corinthians 15:55-57). In the deepest sense he no longer belongs to the realm of death, but the realm of death belongs to him; for it is his stepping-stone to the full realization of the goal of his existence: the glory of God.

In this connection it is instructive to observe the comforting manner in which Scripture speaks of the death of believers. That death is: "precious in the sight of Jehovah" (Psalm 116:15); "a being carried away by the angels into Abraham's bosom" (Luke 16:22); "a going to Paradise" (Luke 23:43); "a going to the house with many mansions" (John 14:2); "a blessed departure" (Philippians 1:23; II Timothy 4:6); in order "to be with Christ" (Philippians 1:23); "to be at home with the Lord" (II Corinthians 5:8); "a gain" (Philippians 1:21); "better by far" (Philippians 1:23); and "a falling asleep in the Lord" (John 11:11; I Thessalonians 4:13).

FOR DISCUSSION

A. *Based on This Chapter*

1. How many persons die every minute in the United States, on the average?

2. Is death a merely natural phenomenon, a mere physical necessity? What is it really?

3. Describe several non-Christian attitudes to death, and criticize them.

4. Why is the Christian attitude entirely different? What is it?

5. In what terms does the Bible describe the death of believers?

B. *Further Discussion*

1. Should a doctor tell "the whole truth" to the patient who faces death?

2. Is death inevitable for all human beings?

3. Are mercy-deaths permissible?

4. Did God actually carry out the threat found in Genesis 2:17? If so, how?

5. Did Jesus die a physical, spiritual, or eternal death?

Chapter 6

A Secret of Unfathomable Depth. What Is It?

Read Psalm 103

1. The Great Riddle

What is that which in a sense has nothing, yet is more precious than the whole world? That which is larger than the sky and deeper than the ocean, yet has never been seen? That which is able to assert itself most vigorously in the very act of denying its own existence? That which is the eye that sees, the mirror through which it sees, and the eye that is seen, all in one? That which can be powerful enough to rule an empire, yet utterly unable to rule itself? That which vaunts itself to be a master, when in reality it is a slave? That which can be a haunt of demons or else a dwelling-place of God? That which, in a sense, holds within its grasp the past, the present, and the future, yet finds rest only in the One who is exalted above every limitation of time?

Can you guess the answer? Well, you will need to have the answer in order to find the answer! But in order to make it easier for you to find the answer, I would suggest that you reread the aforementioned questions and examine them in the light of such passages as the following: Psalm 103:1, 2, 22; Luke 12:19-21; Matthew 16:26; Acts 17:28; Matthew 12:43-45; II Corinthians 6:16 and Deuteronomy 33:27.

Whatever be the answer, it is indeed a secret of unfathomable depth.

2. Is It True That Man Consists of Three Parts: Body, Soul, and Spirit?

Before me lies a book with the title, *The Spirit World,* by C. Larkin. The author says that man is a trinity, and is composed of body, soul, and spirit. He clears up what he means by giving us a diagram. Here are three concentric circles. The outer circle represents man's body; the intermediate, his soul; the innermost or central circle, his spirit. Larkin's proofs for the theory that man consists of three parts are the following: *a*. Man must be a trinity, for the God in whose image he was created is also a Trinity; *b*. the tabernacle had three parts corresponding to man's body, soul, and spirit; and *c*. mention is made of "your whole spirit, soul, and body" in I Thessalonians 5:23, and of "the dividing asunder of soul and spirit" in Hebrews 4:12. All this, he says, proves that man has indeed a spirit and a soul as well as a body.

Maybe you are wondering what this has to do with the Doctrine of the Last Things. You will soon discover the connection.

The doctrine of "the soul's immortality" belongs to a discussion of the Last Things. But we shall never be able to enter upon that subject unless we know what is meant by the terms that are used. An illustration will make this clear. The other day a friend and I happened to be talking to a very learned and amiable brother in the Lord. He told us that he does not believe in *the immortality of the soul*. Now, if anyone makes such a startling statement in your presence, do not at once accuse him of gross heresy. It is always possible that the difference between your belief and his belief is mainly a matter of terminology. So it happened to be also in this case. At first we thought that his denial of the general proposition, "The human soul is immortal" resulted from the fact that he was using the term *immortal* in the strictly biblical sense. That, however, was not the case. It was his understanding of the meaning of the term *soul* that caused a preliminary misunderstanding. This man, just like Larkin, was a *trichotomist,* that is, a believer in the theory that man consists of three parts (over against the belief of the *dichotomist,* namely, that man consists of two parts). As he saw it, within the human personality *the soul* is that which imparts physical life to the body. When the body dies, the soul naturally dies along with it, just as does the soul of an animal at death. But *the spirit* survives!

However, nowhere does Scripture teach that man is composed of three parts. Read Genesis 2:7, and you will notice that in the story of man's creation his *twofold* nature is clearly asserted. A

long list of passages could be given to indicate that the inspired
authors of the Bible were dichotomists. The list would include
such passages as Ecclesiastes 12:7; Matthew 10:28; Romans 8:10;
I Corinthians 5:5; 7:34; Colossians 2:5; and Hebrews 12:9. The
fact that man was created in the image of God, if pressed as
proof for the trichotomist theory, would lead one to the foolish
conclusion that man, as well as God, consists of three *persons*.
Reference to the tabernacle with its three divisions is certainly
far-fetched. As to I Thessalonians 5:23, here the terms *spirit,
soul,* and *body* must not be added up, as if spirit and soul were
two separate entities. (For a translation and interpretation of
that passage see my *Commentary on I and II Thessalonians,* pp.
141, 146-150.) Besides, everywhere else Paul clearly refers to
the human personality as consisting of two parts. And as to
Hebrews 4:12, Prof. Berkhof states, "Hebrews 4:12 should not be
taken to mean that the word of God, penetrating to the inner
man, makes a separation between his soul and his spirit...
but simply as declaring that it brings about a separation in both
between the thoughts and intents of the heart" (*Systematic Theology,* p. 195).

3. What, Then, Is the Soul, and What Is the Spirit of Man?

Both terms refer to that part of the human personality which
is immaterial and invisible. There is only *one* such element,
even though *at least* two names are given to it. Now, it is true
that when the Bible is referring to that immaterial element in
its relation to the body, to bodily processes and sensations, and
in fact to this entire earthly life, with its feelings, affections, likes
and dislikes, it *generally* employs the term *soul (psuche);* for
example, "The Jews stirred up *the souls* of the Gentiles" (Acts
14:2). It is also true that when the reference is to the same
immaterial element considered as the object of God's grace and
as the subject of worship, the term *spirit (pneuma)* is used *most
frequently (always in Paul* when that meaning is intended); for
example, "*My spirit prays*" (I Corinthians 14:14). But the matter
is by no means as simple as that. *In several instances* the two
terms *soul* and *spirit* are used interchangeably, with no (or very

slight) difference in connotation. Let me give one clear example. It is Luke 1:46, 47:

"My *soul* (*psuche*) magnifies the Lord,

And my *spirit* (*pneuma*) rejoices in God my Savior."

And this is only one of several examples that could be given. The conclusion, therefore, is this: When you are talking about man's invisible and immaterial element, you have a perfect right to call it either *soul* or *spirit*. And if anyone, in speaking to you, should maintain that man's *soul* is necessarily his *lower*, immaterial substance, not nearly as valuable as his *spirit*, you might ask him whether he does not believe in *soul*-winning, whether he does not believe that his *soul* is saved, and whether he also does not agree that it were better for a man to forfeit the whole world and not lose his *soul*. When you have made your point clear, suggest to him that he and you sing the hymn, "O *my soul*, bless thou Jehovah!" (Psalm 103).

FOR DISCUSSION

A. *Based on This Chapter*

1. What is a dichotomist and what is a trichotomist?

2. Prove that according to the Bible man consists of two—not three—parts.

3. In the Bible, does the word *soul* always have a different meaning than the word *spirit*?

4. In Scripture, when *soul* has one meaning and *spirit* another, do these two words then indicate two different, immaterial substances dwelling in man? What is the distinctive meaning of each term in cases in which a distinct meaning must be ascribed to each?

5. What has all this to do with the Doctrine of the Last Things?

B. *Further Discussion*

1. You have been studying that riddle with which the present Outline begins. What is your answer?

2. Those who are always referring to I Thessalonians 5:23 and Hebrews 4:12, to prove that the authors of the Bible divided the human personality into three parts, are committing a basic error in Bible-interpretation. What basic rule of interpretation are they forgetting?

3. What do you think of this argument against the position of the trichotomists? If man consisted of *three* parts, he would be able to feel

or sense all three! Also, if man consists of *body, soul* and *spirit,* where does *the heart* come in?

4. Does Scripture urge us to be *soul-winners?* Refer to some passages if you are able to do so.

5. On the basis of Scripture, what methods of soul-winning would you suggest? Is soul-winning the ultimate purpose of our life? In the light of Psalm 103, what is that ultimate purpose? How is soul-winning related to it?

Chapter 7

Does the Soul Survive Death?

Read John 11:17-26

1. The Question Defined

The question at this point is not, "Will the dead live again?" There are those who believe that the dead will indeed live again but deny that the soul survives death! To be sure, this is a strange theory, but it is held by some people.

Neither is the question now, "When a man dies, does his soul survive *in a state of consciousness?* That question, too, is very interesting and will be considered in a future chapter.

The present question is simply this, "When a man dies, does his soul survive?"

2. The Arguments of Those Who Answer the Question Negatively

I am not thinking now primarily of materialists. We all know that the out-and-out materialist teaches that the thought-process or the human "soul" is the secretion of the brain, as bile is the secretion of the liver; and that, accordingly, just as the production of bile ceases when the liver dies, so also the thought-process ceases when the brain stops functioning. But it is not our purpose to pay much attention to these materialists. In their desire to reduce everything to matter they are rejecting the universal testimony of nature and of the senses. Besides, they do not even claim to stand on the same platform with us, for they *reject* the Bible, while we *accept* it.

I am thinking especially of the Russellites, the Watch Tower people, International Bible Students, Jehovah's Witnesses, Millennial Dawnists, or by whatever name they may be called in your community. These people claim that they believe in Scripture. Nevertheless, they reject the idea of survival after death.

Thus, according to J. F. Rutherford, "the thief (of Luke 23:40-43) went *out of existence* (italics are mine), and must remain dead until the resurrection" *(Heaven and Purgatory, p. 23)*. And if you refer to the fact that Jesus told this penitent thief, "Verily I say unto thee, Today thou shalt be with me in Paradise," Rutherford answers that the proper translation or interpretation of that passage is really this: "On this day I solemnly put a question to you, Shall you be with me in Paradise?" (same pamphlet, p. 21).

Constant reference is made, of course, to such passages as Ecclesiastes 3:19, 20; 9:2, 3, 5, 10. Now, according to these passages, the same thing happens to both men and beasts, in that they all die, and the dead know nothing. "This is an evil among all things that are done under the sun, that there is one event for all."

3. Answer

Let no one scare you with these quotations from the book of Ecclesiastes. That book speaks of *goads* and *nails* (Ecclesiastes 12:11). There are those who interpret *the goad* as being *the problem,* viewed as a stimulus to earnest reflection, and *the nail* as *the solution,* which is *nailed down* in this or that observation of wisdom. The goad, according to that interpretation, would be that which perplexes the man who looks at things from the standpoint of the earth ("under the sun"). Well, *as it looks from here,* is it not true that men and beasts all die, and that when they die they lose all direct contact with this world? Are they not all the same in that respect? — But there is also *a nail,* a solution. Viewed from the region above the sun, the author of Ecclesiastes knows that the lot of the righteous is not the same as that of the wicked (Ecclesiastes 2:26). Also, he knows that there is, indeed, a life after death. Man's spirit does not go *out of existence.* On the contrary, "Then shall the dust return to the earth as it was: *and the spirit shall return to God who gave it"* (Ecclesiastes 12:7).

Dr. G. Ch. Aalders, in his excellent commentary on Ecclesiastes, commenting on 9:10b, says, "Does this saying mean to exclude all activity from the life after this life? Not any more than the saying of our Savior recorded in John 9:4 ("Night is approaching when no man can work"). Such expressions refer only to the cessation of all 'toil under the sun,' that is, of all human activity here on earth" (*Commentaar op het Oude Testament,* p. 205).

And what shall we say with respect to Rutherford's translation or interpretation of Christ's word to the penitent thief? How utterly childish! Jesus, then, is supposed to have said, "Verily I say unto thee today." Well, of course, he said it *today.* When else would he be saying it? And as to the suggestion that after the solemn introduction, "Verily I say unto thee," Jesus *asked a question,* and did not follow up his introductory words with *a solemn declaration,* as he does in every similar instance, where is there even the slightest ground for such a thoroughly ridiculous notion?

4. Positive Scriptural Evidence for the Position That the Soul Survives Death

From the section which was read at the beginning of this lesson (John 11:17-26) it became evident that Jesus assured Martha that *believing* is followed by *living,* and that *living and believing* is followed by *never dying.* "Everyone who lives and believes in me *shall never, never die.*" We agree, of course, that the continued life of which Jesus here speaks *is far more than mere continued existence.* But, at least, it *implies* continued existence, which is all we are interested in just now.

Let us now return to Ecclesiastes, the very book from which the Russellites love to quote. The passage which we have in mind is 3:11, "He has set eternity in their heart" (thus rendered in the text of the American Standard Version; see a similar translation in the Revised Standard Version. The new Dutch rendering has "Ook heeft Hij de eeuw in hun hart gelegd"). If this rendering be correct, the passage would mean that man's soul reaches out for the life after this life. But even if, with Dr. G. Ch. Aalders, a slightly different rendering should prove to be the correct one, so that the passage would mean that God has placed in man's soul the urge to reflect or meditate on whatever happens during the course of time (*op. cit.,* p. 77), the *main* conclusion would be the same, namely, that according to *the solution* arrived at even by the author of Ecclesiastes, *man is not in every respect like the beast.* Man has a reflecting, meditating soul; the beast has not.

Then take Exodus 3:6 in the light of Matthew 22:32. It is clear, is it not, that (according to the words of our Lord) Abraham, Isaac, and Jacob were definitely alive, even though their bodies were in the grave. They were destined for the day of the resurrection.

The Parable of the Rich Man and Lazarus (Luke 16:19-31) teaches that both these characters are alive immediately after death. Neither of them has gone "out of existence."

Hebrews 11:13-16 shows that the heroes of faith had considered themselves "strangers and pilgrims on the earth," and that they had been seeking and actually reached the heavenly country which God had prepared for them. Indeed, even at this very moment there is in existence "the general assembly and church of the first-born who are enrolled in heaven." *There* live also "the spirits of just men made perfect" (Hebrews 12:23).

There are many more Scripture passages which prove that the soul survives the body. We shall refer to some of them in future chapters.

FOR DISCUSSION

A. *Based on This Chapter*

1. What is the question which we are seeking to answer in this chapter?

2. What are the arguments of those who deny the soul's survival?

3. How do you answer these arguments?

4. What evidence does the Old Testament offer for the position that the soul survives the death of the body?

5. What evidence for this position does the New Testament offer?

B. *Further Discussion*

1. Would you consider the general resurrection at the end of the age to be proof for the survival of the soul after death?

2. Did Jesus go "out of existence" when he died? See Luke 23:46.

3. Did Stephen go "out of existence" when he died? See Acts 7:59.

4. What happened to Elijah when his life on earth was finished? Did he go "out of existence"? Do you think he found anyone else in heaven besides God and Enoch?

5. What is the practical significance of the doctrine discussed in this lesson?

Chapter 8

Immortality. What Is It? or Is Man Immortal?

Read I Timothy 6:11-16; II Timothy 1:8-12

1. Statements of Different Authors with Respect to Man's Immortality

What do *you* think: Is man immortal or is he not immortal? Opinions differ. One author argues along this line: The idea that the New Testament teaches the soul's immortality is a misunderstanding. The immortality of the soul is a Greek, not a Christian doctrine. The Christian doctrine is that of resurrection not that of immortality. "Immortality, in fact, is only a negative assertion...but resurrection is a positive assertion" (O. Cullmann, "Immortality or Resurrection," an article in *Christianity Today,* July 21, 1958, pp. 3-6).

Another author agrees with this position in so far that he, too, speaks about "the heresy of man's immortal soul." Nevertheless, he is willing to accept the term *immortality,* provided it be applied only to those who are in Christ. He states, "God can destroy both soul and body in hell. And *immortality* is the word that can be applied only to the state of the glorified saints in Christ" (H. Hoeksema, *In the Midst of Death,* a volume in that author's series of *Expositions on the Heidelberg Catechism,* pp. 98, 99).

We turn now to a widely recognized work on doctrine, namely, L. Berkhof, *Systematic Theology,* pp. 672-678. This author points out that the term *immortality* is not always used in the same sense. He does not go so far, however, as to reject completely the idea that in a sense man is immortal. He states, "Immortality, in the sense of continuous or endless existence, is also ascribed to all spirits, including the human soul. It is one of the doctrines of natural religion or philosophy that, when the body is dissolved, the soul does not share in its dissolution, but retains its identity as an individual being. This idea of the immortality of the soul is in perfect harmony with what the Bible teaches about man; but the Bible, religion, and theology are not primarily interested in this purely quantitative and colorless immortality — the bare continued existence of the soul."

So, there you have it. The first author would substitute the term *resurrection* for *immortality*. The next one says, in substance, that only those who are in Christ are immortal. The last one is of the opinion that in a sense the souls of all men are immortal, but that this is not the immortality in which the Bible is primarily interested.

2. Distinctions That Should Be Kept in Mind

Is man immortal or is he not immortal? It all depends upon what you mean by *immortality*.

In a sense only God is immortal. He is "the only One possessing immortality" (see I Timothy 6:11-16). He alone is life's original Owner and never-failing Fountain. His immortality has been called "an original, necessary, and eternal endowment." In God's being there is no death and not even a possibility of death in any sense whatever. Now *immortality* (Greek *athanasia*) means *deathlessness*. This negative implies the positive. God possesses fulness of life, imperishable blessedness (cf. I Timothy 1:17), the inalienable enjoyment of all the divine attributes.

But although only God is immortal in the sense of being the original Owner and Fountain of life and blessedness, in a derived sense it is also true that believers are immortal. In II Timothy 1:8-12 it is clearly stated that our Savior Christ Jesus on the one hand utterly defeated death, and on the other hand, "brought to light life and immortality [literally *incorruptibility*] through the gospel." As a result of Christ's atonement *eternal* death no longer exists for the believer. *Spiritual* death is vanquished more and more in this life and completely when the child of God departs from his earthly enclosure. And *physical* death has been turned into gain. Christ accomplished all that for his children, on the one hand. On the other hand, he brought to light life and incorruptibility. He brought it to light by exhibiting it in his own glorious resurrection. Most of all, he brought it to light by his promise to them: "Because I live you too shall live" (John 14:19); hence through *the gospel*. This *immortality* transcends by far mere endless existence. Even here and now the believer receives this great blessing in principle. In heaven he receives it in further development. Yet he does not fully receive it until the day of Christ's glorious second coming. Until then the bodies of all believers will be subject to the law of decay and death. *Immortality, that is, imperishable salvation for both soul and body*, belongs to the new heaven and earth. It is an inheritance stored away for all those who are in Christ.

Hence, if a person asks you the question, "Is man immortal?" a good answer would be, "Yes, but only in the sense that his existence never ends; but in the Bible only those are called *immortal* who have everlasting life in Christ Jesus, and are destined to glorify him forever as to both soul and body."

3. Scripture's Doctrine of Immortality and That of Greek Philosophy Contrasted

a. The immortality taught by Plato and others after him applies to men in general. The immortality taught in Scripture (when that term or its synonym is actually used) applies in one sense to God alone; in another sense only to those who are in Christ.

b. The immortality of Greek philosophy is nothing but the soul's inherent indestructibility, its necessary endless existence. The immortality of which the Bible speaks is everlasting blessedness.

c. The immortality of pagan thought applies to the soul alone. The body is regarded as the prison from which at death the soul is delivered. According to Scripture our bodies are not prisons but temples. Hence, the Bible's immortality applies to both the soul and the body of the believer, his entire person.

d. The immortality of which the world speaks is a natural or philosophical concept. The immortality of which God speaks in his Word is (in as far as it applies to man) a redemptive concept.

FOR DISCUSSION

A. *Based on This Chapter*

1. In which sense is it true that only God possesses immortality?

2. In which sense is it true that believers, too, are immortal?

3. If a person asks you the question, "Is man immortal?" what would be a good answer?

4. What literally is the meaning of the word *immortality?* What is its synonym?

5. What are the points of contrast between Scripture's doctrine of immortality and that of Greek philosophy?

B. *Further Discussion*

1. Would you say that Adam and Eve before the fall were immortal? If so, in what sense were they immortal? Are angels immortal? Is the devil immortal?

2. Is it possible for the believer, in his association with people of the world, altogether to avoid using terms in the sense in which the world uses them, when Scripture employs these same terms in a different sense? Think of such terms as immortality, fellowship, love.

3. Old-timers used to speak about "the language of Canaan." What does that mean? Should this be cultivated today?

4. Why is the idea of immortality in the sense of the soul's survival and endless existence not nearly as comforting as Scripture's doctrine of immortality? What were Plato's arguments for "immortality" (in his sense of the term)? What do you think of these arguments?

5. Where does Scripture clearly teach that immortality pertains to the believer's body as well as his soul?

Chapter 9

Where Do the Spirits of Believers Go at Death?

Read Hebrews 12:18-24

1. The Relation of This Question to Those That Were Answered Previously

In preceding chapters it has been indicated that according to Scripture it is appointed unto men once to die. Also, we have learned that for the believer death is gain, and that this is true because of Christ's substitutionary atonement. It has been shown, furthermore, that man consists of two parts, very closely related to each other, namely, body and soul (or, if you prefer, body and spirit). It has been proved that these souls survive physical death and that they exist forever and ever, a truth which is often called "the doctrine of immortality." Nevertheless, as has also been indicated, in the sense in which Scripture employs the term God alone possesses immortality as an original, necessary, and eternal endowment; and, of all men, only those who are in Christ have received from him the gift of secondary or derived immortality by virtue of which they are destined for everlasting blessedness with respect to both soul and body.

Granted that all this is true, and that, accordingly, at death the spirits of believers live on, just *where* do these spirits go? In other words, when God's children die, do their souls go to heaven at once? And has this always been the case?

2. The Reason Why This Subject Must Be Discussed

Ever so many people, who claim to believe in the Bible, are not at all sure that the souls of all believers who have died have gone to *heaven*. We have already contradicted the theory of those who teach that at death these souls simply go "out of existence." But there are others. So, for example, the Roman

49

Catholics believe that the souls of most believers go to purgatory, not at once to heaven. (We shall reserve the subject of *purgatory* for later.) And even among evangelical Protestants there are those who believe that thousands upon thousands of believers did not go directly to heaven at death. Before me lies a little book which contains many fine thoughts. The title is *The Christian After Death*. The author is R. E. Hough, Pastor of the Central Presbyterian Church, Jackson, Mississippi. The booklet is published by the Moody Press, Chicago, Illinois. Now, alongside of the many precious Scripture-truths that are found in this treatise there are also a few ideas with which I, for one, cannot agree. One of them is this, that until the ascension of Christ, the righteous at death went not to heaven but to *paradise* (cf. Luke 23:43). The author's reasoning is as follows: Jesus, by means of his death "changed the abode of the disembodied believer...He unlocked the gate of paradise and set free the mighty host which had been awaiting the hour of his sacrifice that he might lead them triumphantly into heaven" (pp. 42-47). We are told, moreover, that another name for *paradise,* this region of bliss which was *not* heaven, was *Abraham's bosom* (cf. Luke 16:22).

3. The Teaching of Scripture

The author seems to proceed from the premise that when two or more names are used to indicate where the children of God go when they die, there must be more than one place. A different name suggests to him a different place. But would it not be strange that for such a wonderful place as heaven there would be only one name? Why cannot "paradise," "Abraham's bosom," and "heaven" indicate the same place, viewed now from one angle, then from another?

Let us say that while you are traveling along the highway, a pretentious house suddenly comes into view. Now is the English language so poor that there is only one word that can properly describe this sumptuous edifice? Is it not probable that this "house" will be referred to as "residence," "mansion," "dwelling," and perhaps even "palace"? If this is true with respect to earthly objects of splendor or grandeur, why should it not be true with respect to heavenly?

The fact that "heaven" and "paradise" are simply different words that indicate the same place is clear from II Corinthians 12, compare verses 2 and 4. Here we read that someone was caught up to "the third heaven." It may be assumed that the first heaven was that of the clouds, the second that of the stars, the third that of the redeemed. But we immediately notice that the man who, according to verse 2, was said to have been caught up to *heaven* was caught up to *paradise,* according to verse 4. This certainly proves that *heaven* and *paradise* indicate the same place and not two different places. And the same thing holds with respect to *Abraham's bosom.* The fact that at death Abraham's soul went to *heaven* is plainly stated in Scripture (Hebrews 11:10, 16; cf. Matthew 8:11).

That the soul of God's child goes to heaven at death is the clear and consistent teaching of Scripture.

Says the Psalmist: "Thou wilt guide me with thy counsel, and afterward receive me to *glory.* Whom have I in *heaven* but thee..." (Psalm 73:24, 25). Surely the Father's house with its many mansions is *heaven* (John 14:2). Our Lord at his ascension went "into *heaven* itself" (Hebrews 9:24). He went there as "our Forerunner" (Hebrews 6:20). To be "with Jesus" means, accordingly, to be *in heaven.* Now Jesus prayed, "Father, I will that they also whom thou hast given me be *with me* where I am, that they may behold my glory" (John 17:24). That the believer, at death, does not have to wait but goes to that place *immediately* is clear from II Corinthians 5:8: "absent from the body...at home with the Lord." For Paul "to depart" meant "to be with Christ," hence, in heaven (Philippians 1:23). Last but not least, the passage that was read at the beginning of this chapter (Hebrews 12:18-24) assures us that right now "the general assembly and church of the firstborn" is "enrolled in heaven."

FOR DISCUSSION

A. *Based on This Chapter*

1. What is the subject of this chapter, and why must it be discussed?

2. Prove from Scripture that *heaven* and *paradise* indicate the same place.

3. Where did Abraham go when he died? Prove it.

4. Prove from Scripture that in the hereafter heaven is the abode of the soul of God's child.

5. Prove that at death the believer *immediately* goes to heaven.

B. *Further Discussion*

1. Give a fuller explanation of Hebrews 12, especially verses 22-24, than is given in the chapter.

2. Who was that man that was "caught up to the third heaven"?

3. What did that man experience when he was caught up to paradise? See II Corinthians 12:4 and 7. Is there any lesson in this for us?

4. When his life on earth was finished, where did Enoch go? And Elijah?

5. According to the belief of the heathen in Paul's day, what happened to the soul at death? See I Thessalonians 4:13 (discussed on pp. 109-111 of my *New Testament Commentary on I and II Thessalonians*). Contrast the Christian view. How does I Thessalonians 3:13 prove that at death the soul of the believer goes to heaven?

Chapter 10

Are the Souls of the Redeemed in Heaven Conscious or Unconscious?

Read II Corinthians 5:1-8

1. Soul-Sleep, the Theory and the Arguments of Those Who Favor It

Sometime ago I preached to an audience other than my own congregation. An observation made by one of the ladies after the service surprised me. What she said, in substance, was this, "I'm so glad that you cleared up this point about the life in heaven. Now I know that my dear ones are not asleep but awake and rejoicing in the glories of heavenly life." I might say in passing that she had recently been bereaved of two who were very precious to her. "You see," she continued, "I have been wondering about this, especially because Mr.... (the name of a prominent person was mentioned here) has been spreading the idea that those who die in the Lord enter a state of unconsciousness and remain in that state until the day of Christ's second coming and the resurrection."

Of course, I had read about this theory. I knew, for example, that way back in early church history a small sect in Arabia believed in the sleep of the soul; also, that at the time of the Reformation this error was being advocated by some of the Anabaptists; that Calvin had refuted it in his treatise *Psychopannychia;* that during the nineteenth century some of the Irvingites in England had clung to it; and that the Russellites in our own day believe in something akin to it, which, however, really amounts to a "going out of existence." But I did not know that even in conservative Christian circles today that notion was again being advocated, and was confusing the minds of some.

Now, what are the arguments upon which these errorists—for

that is what they are — base their view? They are, in the main, the following:

a. The flow of consciousness is dependent on sense-impressions. For example, I *see* a handsome young man, and I start *thinking* about him; or I see a model house, and in my mind I plan to build one like that some day. Or, again, I *hear* the strains of sparkling music, and in my consciousness I am having a feast. But at death there is a complete break with everything that pertains to the senses. I neither hear nor see nor taste nor feel nor smell anything any more. Hence, it must be that the flow of thoughts ceases too. I lapse into unconsciousness, and until I receive a body again I remain asleep.

b. Scripture often represents death as a sleep (Matthew 27:52; Luke 8:52; John 11:11-13; Acts 7:60; I Corinthians 7:39; 15:6, 18; I Thessalonians 4:13; and cf. also such *Old* Testament passages as Genesis 47:30; Deuteronomy 31:16; II Samuel 7:12). Moreover, it contains many other passages which come very near to saying that the dead have no consciousness (Psalm 30:91; 115:17; 146:4; Eccelesiastes 9:10; Isaiah 38:18, 19).

c. Nowhere in Scripture do we read that anyone who had been raised from the dead related what he had seen or heard in heaven. The reason? He had not seen or heard anything, for he had been unconscious or asleep.

2. Answer

As to the first argument (see [a] above):
The soul of man is by no means merely an instrument of the senses. Consciousness can exist apart from sense-experience. God has no body, neither do the angels have bodies. Nevertheless, both God and the angels have consciousness. A man who is a genius of an organist can have music in his soul without having any organ on which to express it. His musical consciousness is not removed from his soul by taking the organ away from him.

As to the second argument (see [b] above):
Nowhere does Scripture say that *the soul* of the departed one falls asleep. It was *the person* who fell asleep, not necessarily the soul. This comparison of death to sleep is very appropriate; for (1) sleep implies rest from labor; the dead also rest from their

labors (Revelation 14:13); (2) sleep implies a cessation of participation in the activities pertaining to the sphere in which one has been busy during the hours of wakefulness; the dead also are no longer active *in the world which they have left;* and (3) sleep is generally *a prelude to awakening;* the dead also will be awakened. In this connection, the comparison of death to sleep is particularly appropriate with respect to the glorious awakening that awaits those who are in Christ.

To be of any value at all to those who favor the soul-sleep theory, the passages referred to would have to prove that those who have entered heaven do not take part *in the activities of the new sphere* which they have now entered. None of the passages to which these errorists appeal proves in any way that this is the case.

As to the third argument (see [c] above):

Let us suppose that after Lazarus died, the Lord, knowing beforehand that after just a few days he was going to raise his friend from the dead, kept *his* soul in a state of unconscious repose. Would such an exception (and a few similar exceptions) prove the rule? Besides, even if we take for granted that those whom our Lord raised from the dead (including Lazarus) had actually been experiencing, however briefly, the conscious joys of life in heaven, is it at all certain that after their return to the earth they were either *able* or *permitted* to talk about their glorious experiences? See II Corinthians 12:4.

3. The Notion of the Sleep of the Soul Cannot Be Harmonized with Those Many Passages Which Clearly Teach or Imply That in Heaven the Souls of the Redeemed Are Fully Awake

Must I indeed believe:

that the redeemed in heaven are experiencing fulness of joy, pleasures foremore (Psalm 16:11) *while they sleep?*

that they behold God's face in righteousness and are satisfied with beholding his form (Psalm 17:15) *while they sleep?*

that they sit down wth Abraham, Isaac, and Jacob (Matthew 8:11) *in their sleep?*

that the rich man, immediately after death, was in torments, cried, and pleaded (Luke 16) *all in his sleep?* that Lazarus (the one referred to in the parable) was comforted (Luke 16) *in his sleep?*

that those for whom Christ offered his touchingly beautiful highpriestly prayer are actually, in fulfilment of that prayer, beholding his glory (John 17:24) *in their sleep?*

that the glories of heaven, with which the sufferings of this present time cannot be compared, will be revealed to us (Romans 8:18) *while we are fast asleep?*

that we shall see face to face and shall know fully (I Corinthians 13:12, 13) *while we sleep?*

that as soon as we are absent from the body we shall be at home with the Lord, delighting in a fellowship with him better than ever before (II Corinthians 5:8) *while we continue to sleep?*

that death for us, believers, will be gain, better by far than anything we have ever experienced on earth (Philippians 1:21, 23) *though we remain fast asleep?*

that the general assembly and church of the firstborn enrolled in heaven (Hebrews 12:23) *is a congregation of sleepers?*

that throughout all the majestic anthems and choruses of heaven, recorded in the book of Revelation (chapters 4, 5, 7, 12) *we remain fast asleep?*

that the new song will be sung (Revelation 5:9; 14:3) *while the redeemed remain asleep?*

that the souls under the altar cry with a great voice (Revelation 6:10) *in their sleep?*

that his servants will serve him day and night in his temple (Revelation 7:15) *while they are fast asleep?*

and that the souls of the victors are sitting on thrones and are living and reigning with Christ (Revelation 20:4) *doing all of this in their sleep?*

Brother, do you really want me to believe that?

For myself, I believe this:

> "When I in righteousness at last
> Thy glorious face shall see,
> When all the weary night is past,
> *And I awake with thee*
> To view the glories that abide,
> Then, then I shall be satisfied."

FOR DISCUSSION

A. *Based on This Chapter*

1. What is meant by soul-sleep?
2. What are the arguments of those who favor this theory?
3. How do you answer these arguments?
4. Are there people today who accept the soul-sleep theory?
5. Quote some Scriptural passages which clearly teach or imply that the souls of the redeemed in heaven are fully awake.

B. *Further Discussion*

1. What is meant by "our earthly tent-dwelling" (or "the earthly house of our tabernacle") in II Corinthians 5:1? And what is meant by "be dismantled" (or "be dissolved" or "be destroyed")?
2. With reference to the expression "a building from God, a house not made with hands, eternal, in the heavens" there are several theories.

    a. Does this refer to the resurrection body?

    b. To an intermediate body, of very thin texture, which we shall receive as soon as our soul enters heaven?

    c. To the actual physical body of Jesus in heaven, so that the souls of all the redeemed in heaven must be viewed as somehow residing inside that body (as a certain speaker from abroad suggested in a lecture years ago)?

    d. To something else, and if so, what?

3. What does Paul mean when he says that we do not wish to be stripped or unclothed but that we would rather be "clothed upon" (II Corinthians 5:4)?
4. What is meant by "the earnest of the Spirit" and why is this a great comfort (II Corinthians 5:5)?
5. How would you use verses 6-8 of II Corinthians 5 in defense of the view that in heaven the souls of the redeemed are fully conscious?

Chapter 11

What Is the Condition of the Souls in Heaven and What Are They Doing?

Read Revelation 7:9-17

1. Their Condition

Never can it be emphasized strongly enough that the redeemed in heaven between the moment of death and that of the bodily resurrection have not yet attained to ultimate glory. They are living in what is generally called "the intermediate" state, not yet the final state. Though, to be sure, they are serenely happy, their happiness is not yet complete.

On this subject Dr. H. Bavinck expresses himself as follows (my translation):

"The condition of the blessed in heaven, though ever so glorious, bears a provisional character, and this for various reasons:

a. They are now in heaven, and limited to that heaven, and not yet in possession of the earth, which along with heaven has been promised to them as an inheritance.

b. Furthermore, they are bereft of a body, and this bodiless existence is not...a gain but a loss. It is not an increase but a decrease of being, since the body belongs to the essence of man.

c. And finally, the part can never be complete without the whole. It is only in connection with the fellowship of *all* the saints that the fulness of Christ's love can be known (Ephesians 3:18). One group of believers cannot attain to fulness without the other group (Hebrews 11:40)" *(Gereformeerde Dogmatiek,* third edition, Vol. 4, pp. 708, 709).

With this we are in hearty accord. But that does not mean that between this intermediate state and the final state (after the resurrection) there is a complete break, a total contrast. On the contrary, just as there is in many respects a continuity between our life here and our life in heaven immediately after death (see, for example, John 11:26; Revelation 14:13), so also there is continuity between that intermediate state and the final state. It would therefore be definitely wrong to say with respect to the symbols of Scripture which describe the final state that these have nothing at all to tell us with respect to the intermediate state. Jerusalem the Golden belongs indeed to the future but also to the present, in as far as that present foreshadows the future. (That is the position I have maintained in my book *More Than Conquerors, an Interpretation of the Book of Revelation;* see especially pp. 238 and 243, and to which I still adhere.)

With this in mind it is therefore entirely legitimate to use Revelation 7:9-17 as a basis for a study of the intermediate state.

Now many of the traits found here in Revelation 7 are of a negative character. We learn that the redeemed are delivered from every care and hardship, from every form of trial and persecution: no more hunger, thirst, or heat. Yet, there are also positive traits. The Lamb is their Shepherd. This Lamb leads his flock to life's springs of water. This water symbolizes eternal life, salvation. The *springs* of water indicate the source of life, for through the Lamb the redeemed have eternal and uninterrupted fellowship with the Father. Finally, the sweetest touch of all: "And God shall wipe every tear out of their eyes." Not only are the tears wiped, or even wiped *away;* they are wiped *out* of the eyes, so that nothing but perfect joy, bliss, glory, sweetest fellowship, abundant life, remains. And God himself is the Author of this perfect salvation.

2. Their Activity

a. *They rest.* See Revelation 14:13. The body, to be sure, is at rest in the grave, waiting the day of the resurrection. But even the soul now rests from life's competition, its toil, sorrow, pain, its mental anguish and especially its sin!

b. *They see Christ's face.* See Revelation 22:4. (Of course, this will be true in an even fuller sense after the resurrection.) The eyes of the redeemed (yes, even the souls have eyes; who will deny it?) are directed to Christ, as the revelation of the Triune God. Here on earth our eyes are often turned away from Christ. One is reminded of the famous painting by Goetze ("Despised and Rejected of Men"), in which you notice how all the eyes are turned away from the spear-riven and thorn-crowned Savior. But in heaven our Lord will be the very center of interest and attention, for *he* will be all-glorious, and *we* will no longer be self-centered. We will not be able to turn our eyes away from him.

c. *They hear.* Will they not hear the glorious choruses and anthems described in the book of Revelation? Will not each of the redeemed hear what all the other redeemed, what the angels, and what Christ have to tell them?

d. *They work.* "His servants shall serve him." There will be a great variety of work, as is clear from such a passage as Matthew 25:21, and by inference also from I Corinthians 15:41, 42. It will be willing *service,* gladly rendered. Do not say that this service is impossible as long as the souls are without their bodies. Are not the angels — who also have no bodies — sent out *to do service?*

e. *They rejoice.* Because every task will be so thoroughly satisfying and refreshing, the redeemed sing while they work. This singing too will, of course, be different after the resurrection. Yet, is it not possible for *souls* to praise God? Is it not possible for the redeemed to have "melodies in their hearts?" Moreover, they have entered into "the joy *of their Lord!*"

f. *They live.* Even during the intermediate state the redeemed actually *live.* They are not day-dreaming. We must not conceive of these souls as silent shadows gliding by. No, they live and rejoice in an abundant and glorious fellowship (about which we hope to say more later, in chapter 13). Moreover, it is *with Christ* that they live. Wherever you find *him,* you will find *them.* Whatever *he* does *they* do (in as far as this is possible for them to do). Whatever *he* has, he shares with *them.* If you wish proof see Revelation 3:12; 3:21; 4:4; cf. 14:14; 14:1; 19:11; cf. 19:14; 20:4.

g. *They reign.* They share with Christ in his royal glory.

FOR DISCUSSION

A. *Based on This Chapter*

1. How does the intermediate state differ from the final state of blessedness; that is, in what three respects?

2. Is there then no connection between the intermediate and the final state?

3. What is the picture drawn in Revelation 7 with respect to the condition of the redeemed in glory?

4. What does it mean that the redeemed rest, see Christ's face, hear, and work or serve?

5. What does it mean that they rejoice, live, and reign?

B. *Further Discussion*

1. How do you explain "the great multitude, which no man could number" described in Revelation 7:9?

2. What is the meaning of the white robes and of the palms?

3. What is the meaning of their song (Revelation 7:10)?

4. Explain Revelation 7:14.

5. We have said very little about the meaning of the redeemed *reigning with Christ* (Revelation 20:4). Explain more fully.

Chapter 12

Is There Direct Contact between the Dead and the Living?

Read Deuteronomy 18:9-15; Hebrews 11:39—12:2

1. There Are Those Who Believe That There Is Some Kind of Direct Contact, Either from One Side or from Both Sides

Do the spirits of the departed ones see us? Can they get into contact with us? Are we able to contact them?

a. *The Spiritualists.* Well, what about Margaret and Kate Fox, respectively fifteen and twelve years of age when *it* happened? What happened? Well, let their mother tell the story of what presumably occurred March 30 of the year 1848:

"The noises were heard in all parts of the house.... We heard footsteps in the pantry and walking downstairs. We could not rest, and then I concluded that the house was haunted by some unhappy, restless spirit." On Friday night, March 31 the mystery repeated itself. Mrs. Fox continues: "My youngest child Cathie, said: 'Mr. Splitfoot, do as I do,' clapping her hands. The sounds instantly followed her with the same number of raps. ...Then Margaret said in sport: 'Now do as I do. Count one, two, three, four,' striking the one hand against the other at the same time; and the raps came as before. She was afraid to repeat them."

According to *Spiritualism,* then, there is such a thing as direct contact between the departed ones and those still dwelling on earth.

b. *The Roman Catholics.* As is well known, they *venerate* "the saints" in heaven, and crave their intercession; saying, for example, *"Sancta Maria, ora pro nobis"* (Holy Mary, pray for us). But are the saints actually able to hear these supplications? Among Roman Catholic divines opinions differ with respect to this point. According to some, the angels serve as intermediaries, informing the saints about the contents of the requests that arise from the earth. According to others God tells the saints all about this matter; or else the saints read these supplications in the mind of God. But still others believe that the spirits of the saints are able to move so quickly from place to place that they have no need of any special informers. This amounts to a kind of direct contact, therefore.

c. *Some Protestants.* But, strange to say, even among soundly evangelical Protestants there are and have been those who accept some kind of direct contact, namely, in the sense that the departed ones who are now in heaven actually see us, and know, *by means of this direct contact,* exactly what we are doing. One is somewhat surprised to find in the company of those who hold this view one who through his writings and his preaching has been, indeed, a great blessing to the church, none other than Clarence Edward Macartney. In a sermon on Hebrews 12:1 ff, he commented on the expression "we are compassed about with so great a cloud of witnesses" as follows:

"That the dead observe us and are conscious of what we do in this life seems to be the reasonable inference from that great verse," and again, "I have little doubt that they observe our life here in this world" *(More Sermons from Life,* p. 199, then 197).

2. Scripture Rejects This Idea

The Bible is completely opposed to this idea of any direct contact between the departed and those left behind.

As to a. *the Spiritualists:* Not only is communion between the two groups impossible but the attempt to effect it is strictly forbidden by the Lord; see Deuteronomy 18.

As to b. *the Roman Catholics:* Though Scripture everywhere urges us to intercede for one another (Romans 15:30; Ephesians 6:18, 19; Colossians 1:2, 3; I Timothy 2:1, 2; etc.), and teaches us that God often sends deliverance in answer to such prayers of intercession (Exodus 32:11-14; Numbers 14:13-20; cf. Genesis 18); nowhere does it in any way admonish us to ask for the intercession of those who have departed from this life, and nowhere does it imply that these departed ones are able to see and to hear what we are doing.

In fact, the very opposite is clearly implied. According to Scripture, those who have died *are asleep* with respect to the realm which they have left behind (as was pointed out previously). Whether their children are getting rich or are remaining poor is not known to them (Job 14:21). From their heavenly mansions neither Abraham nor Jacob is able to see or hear what is happening here below to their descendants (Isaiah 63:16; cf. also Ecclesiastes 9:10). It is hardly necessary to add that the *veneration* of the saints, which so easily degenerates into actual adoration and worship, is a form of idolatry, strictly forbidden by Scripture.

As to c. *Some Protestants.* The explanation of Hebrews 12:1, 2 that is offered by Clarence Edward Macartney is incorrect. For the correct interpretation see H. Bavinck *(Gereformeerde Dogmatiek,* Vol. IV, 3rd ed., page 689), and also the fine comments on this passage in popular commentaries on Hebrews by such men as J. C. Macaulay and W. H. Griffeth Thomas; and cf. Erich Sauer, *In the Arena of Faith,* p. 76. Says the latter:

"The expression 'witness' scarcely means that these men of God are *spectators...*of our present race and strife. It is not as though they watch from their exalted seats the battle in the *arena* here below. There are no scriptures which tell us that those who have left this earthly life take an active, conscious part in the things concerning the church militant. They [the faith-heroes of Hebrews 11] are characterized here as people who gave witness in their generation, and who, when we examine their life, are an example for us today of *faith in action,* winning victories in God. Although death has taken them away from this scene, their testimony remains. So that by this means and in this sense these heroes of faith of yesterday are, as it were, present with us today. In fact they *compass us about* and encourage us in the faith."

FOR DISCUSSION

A. *Based on This Chapter*

   1. What is the question discussed in this chapter?

2. What do the Spiritualists (or Spiritists) believe? Tell the story of the Fox family.

3. What is the Roman Catholic belief and practice with respect to this matter?

4. How did the Rev. Clarence Edward Macartney interpret Hebrews 12:1, 2?

5. What does Scripture teach on this entire subject?

B. *Further Discussion*

1. I have told you only the beginning of the Fox family story. Can you tell the rest of it?

2. Why is the Roman Catholic doctrine of the veneration of the saints dangerous? I mean this: What does veneration of the saints do to adoration and worship of the Triune God through Christ?

3. In the chapter the point was established that there is no *direct* contact between those left behind and those who have departed from us. Is there any *indirect* contact? If so, prove this from the Bible.

4. If there be no direct contact between the militant and the triumphant church, in which sense is it true, nevertheless, that the two meet each other?

5. What is the best way to honor those who have gone home to be with the Lord?

Chapter 13

Shall We Know Each Other There?

Read Luke 16:1-9

1. Is the Desire To-Meet-One-Another-Again Right?

Shall we recognize each other in heaven? How often has not this question been asked! Some freely express their yearning to renew those happy associations broken off on earth when a dear one passed on. Others, however, are somewhat more hesitant in speaking about this matter. They wonder whether the desire for meeting-one-another-again (German *Wiedersehen* - Dutch *Wederzien*) is even right. Is not the chief end of man "to glorify God and enjoy *him* forever"? And did not the Psalmist (Psalm 73:25) exclaim:

"Whom have I in heaven *but thee?*"

The answer would seem to be this: All *such* yearning for mutual recognition and re-association which is of a merely sentimental character, failing to accord to God in Christ the chief honor, must be condemned. But the desire for *Wiedersehen* itself, in order that in company with those who have preceded us and with those who are to follow us we may praise our Redeemer is entirely legitimate. In fact, we were created *for fellowship*. Accordingly, I am in complete agreement with Dr. H. Bavinck, who says (in his *Gereformeerde Dogmatiek*, third edition, Vol. IV, pp. 707, 708, my translation): "The hope to-see-one-another-again on the other side of the grave is entirely natural, genuinely human, and also in harmony with Scripture. For, the latter does not teach the kind of immortality that is stripped of all content and pertains to phantomic souls, but rather that everlasting life which belongs to real human individuals.... Hence, though it is true that the joy of heaven consists primarily in fellowship with Christ, it also consists in fellowship of believers with each other. And even as on earth the latter type of fellowship, though here always imperfect, does not detract from the believers' fellowship with Christ but strengthens and enriches it, so it will also be in heaven. Paul's chief desire was to depart and be with Christ (Philippians 1:23; I Thessalonians 4:17), but Jesus himself pictures the joy of heaven under the symbolism of a banquet where all will sit at the table with Abraham, Isaac, and Jacob (Matthew 8:11; cf. Luke 13:28). Accordingly, the hope of seeing-each-other-again is not wrong if only it remains subordinate to the longing for fellowship with Christ."

2. Does Scripture Teach That There Will Be Such a Joyous Recognition and Restoration of Fellowship?

In this same great work on Reformed Doctrine Dr. H. Bavinck speaks with commendable caution on many controversial subjects. With respect to the matter of recognition in the life hereafter he is, however, very definite and outspoken. Says he: (*op. cit.*, p. 688) "Without any doubt those who have died recognize those whom they have known on earth."

Those who, along with Dr. H. Bavinck, accept this idea of recognition and restored fellowship usually appeal to the following passages, not all of which furnish *direct* evidence.

a. According to Isaiah 14:12 the inhabitants of Sheol, immediately recognizing the king of Babylon as he descends toward them, mockingly greet him, exclaiming, "How art thou fallen from heaven, O day-star, son of the morning! How art thou cut down to the ground, thou that didst lay low the nations...."

b. According to Ezekiel 32:11 out of the midst of Sheol the mighty heroes address the ruler and the people of Egypt.

c. According to Luke 16:19-31 the rich man recognizes Lazarus.

d. According to Luke 16:9 the friends whom we make for ourselves by our material gifts will welcome us into the mansions of heaven. The sick whom we have visited, the bereaved with whom we have sympathized, the heathen' for whom we have been instruments unto salvation will as it were be standing in the vestibule of heaven in order to receive their benefactors into their circle, so as together to glorify the One who is the source of every blessing. This surely implies recognition and resumption of fellowship.

e. I Thessalonians 2:19, 20 (cf. also II Corinthians 4:14) implies that at the coming of Lord Jesus Christ the missionaries will see the ultimate realization of their hope, and will experience supreme joy when they behold the fruits of their missionary efforts standing there, with gladness, thanksgiving, and praise, at Christ's right hand. And is not restoration of broken fellowship implied in I Thessalonians 4:13-18?

3. Objections Answered

Objection a. Some of the passages listed in support of the theory of recognition and restoration of fellowship have reference to the events that are ushered in by Christ's second coming rather than to the intermediate state. After Christ's return we shall have bodies by means of which recognition can possibly be achieved. But this in no wise proves that right now in heaven the disembodied souls of believers recognize each other.

Answer. There is some merit in this argument, namely, in so far as it points to the fact that a distinction must be made. Surely, after Christ's return, when our bodies, gloriously raised or changed, will have been restored to us, recognition and fellowship will necessarily be far richer. Nevertheless, the contrast between the intermediate and the final state is not so great that what is said here about the final state would not apply even in principle to the intermediate state. Also, some of the passages clearly have reference to the soul *immediately after death*. And besides, if it be possible for angels—who have no bodies—to recognize each other (Daniel 10:13), why should it be deemed impossible for disembodied souls of believers to do likewise?

Objection b. If we should actually *recognize* those of our friends whom we meet in heaven, we would also *miss* those earthly friends, acquaintances or relatives who never arrive in heaven. This would make us very unhappy even in heaven.

Answer. Does not our Lord Jesus Christ miss many a one whom he has sincerely admonished? Would you say, then, that Jesus is unhappy in heaven? Is not the answer rather in this direction, namely, that when once we get to heaven *all such ties as were not in Christ* (including even family ties) will lose their meaning? And does not Matthew 12:46-50 definitely point in that direction?

Objection c. According to Matthew 22:23-33 all earthly relationships will be completely obliterated in the life hereafter. Hence, any recognition of those whom we have known on earth would be meaningless.

Answer. That is not at all what Matthew 22:23-33 teaches. It teaches that since in the life hereafter there will be no more death there will be no marriage relationship nor any need for this. In *that* respect we shall be like the angels in heaven. The passage says nothing whatever about abolition of every relationship with those whom we have known in the Lord while we were on earth.

The belief in *Wiedersehen* in the life hereafter is firmly rooted in Scripture.

FOR DISCUSSION

A. *Based on This Chapter*

1. What is the question discussed in this chapter?

2. Is the desire to-meet-one-another-again in the hereafter a legitimate desire? Why do you think so?

3. Does Scripture support the view that this desire will be fulfilled?

4. But is it possible for disembodied souls to recognize each other?

5. What are the other objections, and how do you answer them?

B. *Further Discussion*

1. Can the fact that Peter, James, and John recognized Moses and Elijah on the Mount of Transfiguration be used as an argument in favor of recognition in the life hereafter?

2. Would you also appeal to I Corinthians 13:12 in support of this view?

3. Someone made the statement, "Not only shall we recognize each other in the life hereafter, but we shall even know each other better than we have ever known each other before." Do you believe that this is true? Why, or why not?

4. What really is *the point* in the Parable recorded in Luke 16:1-9? I refer to the *practical lesson.*

5. What is meant by "the mammon of unrighteousness"? Have you examined the difference between the King James or Authorized Version of Luke 16:9 and the American Standard Version? Which is better on this passage?

Chapter 14

Do Memory, Faith, and Hope Go with Us to Glory? Is There "Time" in Heaven?

Read Revelation 6:9-11

1. Brief Interpretation of the Vision of the Souls under the Altar

What John sees is not heaven itself but a symbolical vision of heaven. Nevertheless the vision would be meaningless if it did not reflect reality. Accordingly, just as we have a right to draw certain conclusions from the parable of the Rich Man and Lazarus, so does the same principle apply here.

Now in this vision John beholds the altar, which here appears as the altar of burnt-offering at the base of which the blood of slaughtered animals had to be poured out (Leviticus 4:7). Underneath this altar John sees the blood of slaughtered saints. He saw *the souls,* for "the soul is in the blood" (Leviticus 17:11). They had offered themselves as a sacrifice, having clung to the testimony which they had received concerning the Christ and salvation in him. Now the souls of these people were crying for vengeance upon those who had slaughtered them.

To each of these slaughtered ones a white, flowing robe is given, symbolizing righteousness, holiness, and festivity. To them is given the assurance that their prayers will be answered but that the time for the judgment has not yet arrived. Hence, these souls must enjoy their repose "for a little time" until every elect has been brought into the fold, and the number of the martyrs is full. God knows the exact number. Until that number has been completed, the day of the final judgment cannot come.

Is not the conclusion warranted that these souls have been resting for some time, are resting now, and must rest a little while longer? States Dr. H. Bavinck, "They have a past which they remember, a present in which they live, and a future which they are approaching" (*Gereformeerde Dogmatiek,* third edition, Vol. IV., pp. 709, 710).

2. Do Memory, Faith, and Hope Go with Us to Glory?

First, as to memory. The rich man in the parable (Luke 16:28) remembers that he has five brothers on earth. In the day of judgment certain wicked individuals remember that they used to prophesy, cast out demons, and perform many mighty works (Matthew 7:22). Have the righteous no memory at all? Even Matthew 25:37-40 does not really teach this, but implies rather the opposite. Moreover, how will the redeemed ever be able to sing the new song, in which they praise God for his wonderful redemptive acts, if they have no memory of these acts? And does not even the singing of this song (Revelation 14:3; 15:3, 4; cf. 5:9) imply a certain movement or progression in time, from the line that has been sung, to the line that is being sung, and thus on toward the line that is about to be sung? Does it not imply *past, present, and future* even in heaven? True indeed, by far the most of the redeemed in glory have no voices until the day of the resurrection. But is singing therefore impossible? Are not glorious refrains ringing in their hearts? Is it not true that even here on earth *"in my heart* there rings a melody...there rings a melody of love"? Call these songs symbols, if you wish, they surely are symbols of something that is very real.

If it has now been established that memory, purified of every sinful stain, but memory, nevertheless, goes with us to heaven, a memory naturally with reference to *the past,* what about the exercise of faith in *this present moment?* It has been argued that:

> "Faith will vanish into sight;
> Hope be emptied in delight.
> Love in heaven will shine more bright,
> Therefore give us love."

Now in a sense it is true that faith will vanish (cf. II Corinthians 5:7). Belief in the promise, considered as still unfulfilled, will be replaced by delight in the fulfilment of that promise. But certainly faith in the sense of *active trust in God* will not be absent from heaven. Will it not shine forth more gloriously than ever, since never again will the anguished cry be heard, "Lord, I believe; *help thou mine unbelief*"?

But what about hope with reference to the future? The fact that hope too goes with us to glory is still the best interpretation of I Corinthians 13:13. Hope, as well as faith and love, *abides* when "that which is perfect is come," and when we shall see "face to face." Even now the spirits of the redeemed in heaven know that this is no more than *the intermediate state.* They are, as it were, reaching forward to the time when they will receive their bodies, gloriously raised, and will be joined by all the others who will one day belong to their number. They are yearning for the time when they will inherit "the new heaven and earth," and when their Lord will be publicly vindicated. It is true what Dr. Johannes G. Vos states in his article "The Intermediate State" *Christianity Today,* May 12, 1958, p. 12): "Scripture represents the intermediate state as provisional, constituting neither the ultimate bliss of the saved nor the ultimate doom of the lost."

In heaven, then, the souls of the redeemed *really live,* thanking God for his blessings in the past, cleaving to him in the present, and anticipating a future still more glorious than the present in which they already rejoice. Life in three tenses, therefore, and this even in glory.

3. **But Does Not This View of the Intermediate State Imply That for Human Individuals There Will Be Time Even in Heaven...and in Hell?**

The idea that *time* in every conceivable sense will be completely absent from the life hereafter has taken firm root in the minds of many. It has been incorporated in the lines of familiar hymns; for example, "And he swore with his hand raised to heaven, that time was no longer to be." If we may rely on the student-notes of the lectures of Dr. A. Kuyper Sr., then this great theologian and statesman spoke with deep conviction on this matter. He was entirely certain that in the intermediate state there would be no time. He relied heavily on Revelation 10:6, to which he refers more than once, "And he sware by him that liveth for ever and ever...that there should be time no longer" (See *Dictaten Dogmatiek, Locus De Consummatione Saeculi,* pp. 102, 103). It is to be deplored that the great theologian failed to make a more critical study of the text on which he relies so heavily. In the light of the context a different translation is surely to be preferred (a translation that differs from that which is found in the *Staten Vertaling* of the Dutch Bible and which agrees substantially with that found in the Authorized Version of our English Bible). The text of both the American Standard Version and of the Revised Standard Version has a far better rendering, namely, "there shall be delay no longer," or "there should be no more delay." The new Dutch translation is similar, *"Er zal geen uitstel meer zijn."*

Personally I am in agreement with Dr. G. Vos who states (with reference to the age to come), "Paul nowhere affirms that to the life of man, after the close of this aeon, no more duration, no more divisibility in time-units shall exist. Life so conceived is plainly the prerogative by nature of the Creator: to eternalize the inhabitants of the coming aeon in this sense would be equivalent to deifying them, a thought whose place is in a pagan type of speculation but not within the range of biblical religion" (*The Pauline Eschatology*, p. 290). Similarly Dr. H. Bavinck states (*op cit.* p. 709), "Those who have died remain finite and limited beings and cannot exist in any other way than in space and time. The measurement of space and the computation of time, to be sure, will be entirely different on the other side of the grave than they are here, where *miles and hours* are our standard of measurement. But even the souls that dwell there will not become eternal and omnipresent like God...They are not raised above every form of time, that is, above time in the sense of a succession of moments."

I wish to stress, however, that I am also in substantial agreement with Dr. Johannes G. Vos, who, in the article already mentioned, states, "J. Stafford Wright has suggested that in the intermediate state the human mind will be geared to a different kind of time-scale from that of the physical universe, though we cannot guess what it might be." He points to the fact that for the souls under the altar the period between their martyrdom and the resurrection at the last day is called "a little season," though it has already lasted a long, long time.

So, when the question is asked, "Is there time in heaven?" namely, in the sense of movement from the past, into the present, into the future—call it *duration* or *succession of moments*—, the answer must be, "Yes." When the further question is asked, "Will it in every respect be time as we now know it (that is, will it be measured by our present earthly standards?), the answer will have to be, "No."

FOR DISCUSSION

A. *Based on This Chapter*

1. Explain the vision of the souls under the altar.
2. Would you say that these souls are living in three tenses?
3. Does memory go with us to heaven?
4. Do faith and hope go with us to heaven?
5. Are the redeemed going to be like God, raised above time in every respect? Will time be measured there as it is measured here?

B. *Further Discussion*

1. How can we justify this cry for vengeance of these souls under the altar?
2. "Where they count not time by years." Do you agree?
3. Will time be the same in heaven as in hell?
4. Is hope possible where there is no time in any sense? Distinguish between hope here and hope there.
5. Why is love called "the greatest of these"?

Chapter 15

Is There Progress in Heaven?

Read II Corinthians 3:12-18 and Ephesians 3:14-21

1. In Heaven There Is No Progress in Sanctification

"Nothing unclean shall enter heaven at all" (see Revelation 21:27). When a believer dies, he is in that selfsame moment wholly delivered from sin in every form. It is clear, therefore, that in the life hereafter there can be no progress in *holiness*. Today Abraham is not any holier than he was the very instant his soul arrived in heaven. In heaven there is no advance in *sinlessness*. In that respect all the redeemed are absolutely *perfect* from the very moment they enter the pearly gates.

2. Nevertheless, There Can Very Well Be Progress in Heaven; for Example in Knowledge, Love, and Joy

I do not know of a single passage in the entire Bible which directly and literally would prove that there is even this kind of progress in heaven. The church has not incorporated this idea in its confessions. If one is inclined to disagree with the theory that there is progress in heaven, he has the perfect right to do so. It is entirely a matter of inference, not of direct and positive proof.

That having been said, it is, nevertheless, the opinion of many— for example, H. Bavinck, J. J. Knap, R. C. H. Lenski, J. D. Jones — that there is such progress. This opinion is based on inference or deduction. Personally I believe that the inference is legitimate. I base my own opinion in the matter on the following grounds:

a. *Scripture's doctrine of everlasting life* (John 3:16; 11:25, 26; especially 10:10). According to Scripture, when the soul enters heaven it continues to live. It does not just remain everlastingly in a fixed position. It does not simply "stay put." It lives more

75

abundantly than ever before. Now *to live* means to think, to have fellowship, to see and hear, to rejoice, etc. Now, as it would seem to me, for finite beings, in a state of sinlessness, such living spells progress. Is it at all probable that we shall think and not advance in *knowledge?* That we shall have fellowship — and what a fellowship! — and not make progress in *love?* That we shall see and hear the glories of heaven and not become enriched in our experience of heavenly *joy?*

Moreover, growth in knowledge, love, and joy is not necessarily inconsistent with "perfection." Just as here on earth the "perfect" child is the growing child, and just as the "perfect" Christ-child was the one who *"advanced* in wisdom and stature, and in favor with God and men" (Luke 2:52), so it may well be in heaven.

b. *Scripture's doctrine of the greatness of God and the little-ness of man* (Isaiah 40:25, 26; 44:6; 45:5). According to Scripture, our souls are—and ever remain—*finite, restricted, limited.* But God in Christ is—and ever remains—*infinite, unrestricted, unlimited.* Besides God there is no God. Now when, in the condition of absence from sin and death, the condition that results from *redemption,* the finite comes into contact with the infinite, is it possible that the finite would not make progress? When the in-exhaustible riches of heaven are poured into vessels of definitely limited capacity, is it possible that such vessels would not become more and more filled?

Take, as an example, Christ's love toward us. Even in heaven we shall strive to know "the breadth, length, height, and depth" of that love. Of course, no redeemed soul will strive to do this all by himself. He will try to do it "together with all the saints." Even then, however, according to Scripture that love of Christ toward us is a love which "passes knowledge." The whole of it will ever remain too great for human comprehension. It is exactly as the poet said:

> "Could we with ink the ocean fill,
> And were the skies of parchment made,
> Were every blade of grass a quill,
> And every man a scribe by trade;
> To write the love of God to man

Would drain the ocean dry,
Nor could the scroll contain the whole,
Though stretched from sky to sky."

That, as I see it, will be the glory of heavenly life; namely, that we shall be delving ever more deeply into that love of God, and shall continue to discover everlastingly that we have not reached bottom and can never reach bottom, *for there is no bottom;* that love is *infinite.* We shall never be told, "Now you know absolutely all there is to know about the love of God in Christ." If thorough, infinite comprehension of God's love — or of any of his attributes — were possible, we would cease to be finite. We would ourselves be God. And yet, besides God there is no God! As long, therefore, as Christ's love remains infinite and we remain finite, we shall make progress in our knowledge of that love and in our loving and joyful response to it. Is it even conceivable that one who — even if only with the eye of his soul — beholds the glory of God in Christ would not advance in knowledge, love, and joy?

c. *Scripture's doctrine of the absence of sin from the realm of heaven* (Matthew 6:10; Revelation 21:27). In heaven, according to Scripture, there is no sin. This means that the chief obstacle to progress will have been completely removed. Neither sin nor the curse is able to dwell there at all. Now it would seem to me that minds unobscured by sin will make better progress in knowledge than minds obscured by sin; that hearts no longer oppressed by the results of sin will advance more readily in inner delight than hearts that are thus oppressed.

d. *Scripture's symbolic language* (I John 3:9; Revelation 22:1, 2; cf. Ezekiel 47:1-5). The Bible pictures everlasting life or salvation under the symbolism of a germinating seed, a growing and fruit-bearing tree, an ever-deepening river, etc. All such figures would seem to imply progress.

e. *Scripture's doctrine of the abiding character of hope* (I Corinthians 13:13). Hope means joyful anticipation of glories still to come. To be sure, here on earth we also hope. But these hopes are not always fulfilled. In heaven, however, every hope attains fulfilment, and, at the same time, hope continues on and on. Does not this twofold fact imply everlasting progress, namely, in knowledge, love, joy, etc.? Indeed, as I see it, there is progress in heaven, and this even during the intermediate state.

FOR DISCUSSION

A. *Based on This Chapter*

1. In which sense is it true that there is no progress in heaven?

2. In which sense could it, nevertheless, be true that there is progress in heaven?

3. Do you think that finite creatures will ever be able to know "all about" the love of Christ? If not, why not?

4. Does the absence of sin from the realm of heaven have anything to do with the possibility of progress in heaven?

5. What are some of the other arguments on which I have based the opinion that there is progress in heaven?

B. *Further Discussion*

1. Purposely I used the expression "progress; *for example,* in knowledge, love, and joy." Can you add anything to this list of three?

2. Adam and Eve were "perfect" before the fall. Did that exclude the possibility of progress?

3. Our Lord Jesus Christ, as man, was "perfect," completely sinless. Did that exclude the possibility of progress? See Hebrews 5:7-10; notice especially verse 8. How do you explain that?

4. Does I Corinthians 13:12 ("then shall I know fully even as I was fully known") exclude any idea of the possibility of progress? Hint: does this actually mean, "then shall I know *infinitely*"? If it meant that, what would that make of us? What does I Corinthians 13:12 mean in the light of the entire context?

5. Is this idea of progress even in heaven of any *practical* value? For instance, is there possibly a relation between our rate of spiritual progress here and our rate of progress (in knowledge, love, joy, etc.) there?

Chapter 16

Do the Wicked Go to Hell When They Die?

Read Psalm 73:12-19

1. A Very Unpopular Doctrine

"Ladies and Gentlemen: The idea of a hell was born of revenge and brutality on the one side, and cowardice on the other....I have no respect for any human being who believes in it. I have no respect for any man who preaches it....I dislike this doctrine, I hate it, I despise it, I defy this doctrine....This doctrine of hell is infamous beyond all power to express." Thus spoke Col. R. G. Ingersoll, "the great agnostic."

Pastor Russell used to hammer away at his favorite subject, "The Nightmare of Eternal Torture." As he saw it, this terrible doctrine was being proclaimed by the ministers of the established churches in order to instill fear in the hearts of their people so that they might remain manageable.

Let me add a statement by a Seventh Day Adventist: "To many people, religion is merely a fire-escape. They have been scared into accepting it by hearing descriptions of a place which burns eternally, and into which they have been told they will be cast at death if they do not get religion and go to church."

2. Objections to the Doctrine of Hell, Together with the Answers

Objection a. God is love. Therefore, the very existence of hell is impossible. "A creator that would torture his creatures eternally would be a fiend, and not a God of love" (Rutherford, *World Distress*, p. 40).

Answer. Love does not exclude wrath, especially for those who stubbornly reject this love. It was Jesus Christ himself, the very embodiment of love, who spoke again and again about the punishment of hell.

Objection b. God is righteousness. Accordingly, he would not visit *temporal* sin with *everlasting* punishment. That would not be fair, for the punishment must match the crime.

Answer. It is not necessarily the duration of the crime that fixes the duration of the punishment. Even now a crime committed within a minute may earn a life-sentence. What is decisive is the nature of the crime. An act of treason against one's country is often punished with death. Hence, treason against the highest Majesty, wilful rejection of the God of love, merits the extreme penalty.

Objection c. God is righteousness (once more). Hence he would not plunge into the deepest hell millions upon millions of innocent pagans who have never even heard the gospel.

Answer. Since a separate chapter (chapter 20) will be devoted to this subject, it will be omitted here.

Objection d. God is wisdom. Hence, he knows that extreme punishment would not accomplish anything useful.

Answer. What matters is that God remain God! Else all is lost for everybody. God cannot remain God unless his attributes —including his justice—be maintained. "Let justice be maintained though the world perish." Abrogation of this principle would mean the end for both God and man. Now it was the inexorable maintenance of God's justice that nailed Jesus to the cross as the Savior from sin. Moreover, God threatens with the most intense punishment those who reject such a loving and wonderful Savior. When, in conjunction with the promise of salvation for all who accept Christ, this threat is taken seriously, an immeasurable influence for good is exerted upon men. Moreover, God's honor is maintained, and his justice is satisfied. And that, after all, is the thing that matters most.

Objection e. God is omnipotence (and love). Therefore he will not permit Satan to keep in his grasp those whom he (God) has created. A certain minister with universalistic convictions expressed it somewhat differently. He was preaching in a supposedly conservative church, and I was in the audience. His statement was this, "In the end everybody will be saved. I have hope even for the devil."

Answer. God does not use his almighty power to drag men to heaven, in such a manner that their own responsibility would cease. A man who wilfully rejects Christ is lost because of his own sin.

With respect to the proposition that in the end all men, demons, and even Satan himself will be saved, Scripture teaches the very opposite (Matthew 7:13, 14; 22:14; 25:10; 25:41; 25:46; Jude 6).

Objection f. God is the Creator. He has so created us that we instinctively rebel against the idea of everlasting punishment. Hence, this idea cannot be true, for "the voice of the people is the voice of God."

Answer. The rejection of the idea of everlasting punishment springs not from creation but from rebellion. And surely *after the fall* the slogan, "The voice of the people is the voice of God" is in need of considerable qualification. Man, prompted by his evil nature, prefers Barabbas to Christ.

Objection g. God is the Revealer. In his Word he does not teach that the wicked go to hell when they die.

Answer. We are now getting to the very heart of the matter. The question is not whether Ingersoll or anyone else dislikes, hates, despises, and defies the doctrine of hell but whether God in his Word has revealed it. This leads us now to the final subheading:

3. Does the Bible Really Teach That the Wicked Go to Hell When They Die?

Here we must be careful. Very often when Scripture speaks about the eternal destiny of the wicked, it is discussing their *final* state, that is, their punishment *as to both body and soul after the judgment day.* Special chapters will be devoted later on to this subject (chapters 46, 47). But here we are only dealing with the question whether the wicked go to hell *when they die.*

Scripture's teaching on this point, though not extensive, is clear enough. A few illustrations must suffice. According to Asaph, when the wicked die they are plunged into ruin. They become a desolation in a moment. They are swept away utterly by *terrors* (Psalm 73:12-19). When "the rich man" dies, he descends to a place of *torments,* from which there is *no escape* (Luke 16:23, 26). And when Judas committed suicide, he went "to his own place," the place of perdition naturally (Acts 1:25).

FOR DISCUSSION

A. *Based on This Chapter*

1. What did Ingersoll say about the doctrine of hell?

2. What do the Russellites — Jehovah's Witnesses — say about it?

3. And the Seventh Day Adventists?

4. What objections are advanced against the doctrine of hell, and how can these objections be answered?

5. Does the Bible teach that the wicked go to hell when they die?

B. *Further Discussion*

1. Is it possible to be on the wrong side with respect to the doctrine of hell, but on the right side with respect to the doctrine of redemption through Christ?

2. Russellites used to call themselves "International Bible Students." But is the Bible really basic in their thinking? What is basic?

3. Are we in our own circles guilty of *over*-emphasizing the doctrine of everlasting punishment? Of *under*-emphasizing it?

4. Is the following correct *and complete*: According to the author of Psalm 73 the wicked prosper greatly in this life, while the righteous are afflicted. But *in the end* the tables are turned? See especially verses 23 and 24.

5. Those who say that the doctrine of hell is inconsistent with God's love, and that, accordingly, there is no hell, face still another difficulty, not mentioned in the chapter. What is it?

Chapter 17

What Is Meant by Sheol and Hades?

Read Luke 16:19-31

1. Four Erroneous Views with Respect to Sheol

You may well wonder why an entire chapter is devoted to this subject. Why bother about the meaning of a Hebrew word and a Greek word? Why not take up something "more practical"? The reason is this: just now it is very practical and useful to know whatever there is to be known with respect to the meaning of these two strange words, the Old Testament *Sheol* and the New Testament *Hades,* for certain sects are constantly telling the people that due to a wrong translation of these words (and of *Gehenna)* the doctrine of *hell* as a place of everlasting punishment has taken such a hold in the church. And so these sects emphasize that if only people would take the time to examine what these words really mean *in the original,* peace of soul would be restored.

Well, let us then follow their advice, and study these two words as thoroughly as is possible in one chapter (reserving *Gehenna* for chapter 46).

Sheol occurs more than sixty times in the Old Testament. In the Greek translation of the Old Testament (referred to as LXX) it is generally rendered Hades, which is also the New Testament equivalent. Hence, Sheol and Hades should be studied together. Now the Authorized Version, struggling with the problem of finding a good rendering for Sheol, uses "pit" in only three instances (Numbers 16:30, 33; and Job 17:16). Elsewhere its rendering is divided about equally between "hell" and "grave." You will find the rendering "hell" in the following passages: Deuteronomy 32:22; II Samuel 22:6; Job 11:8; 26:6; 7:27; 9:18; 15:11, 24; 23:14; 27:20; Isaiah 5:14; 14:9, 15; 28:15, Psalm 9:17; 16:10; 18:5; 55:15; 86:13; 116:3; 139:8; Proverbs 5:5;

18; 57:9; Ezekiel 31:16, 17; 32:27; Amos 9:2; Jonah 2:2; and Habakkuk 2:5).

Now the first erroneous view would be the belief that the Authorized (or King James) Version is always right in its rendering of Sheol. When the Russellites point to "errors in translation" they are right *in part.* Anyone can see this for himself. For example, did the author of Psalm 116 really mean to say that "the pains of *hell*" had gotten hold of him? Does Isaiah, in the original and according to the context, actually intend to tell us that the multitude of captives, together with their pomp and glory, descended into *hell* (see Isaiah 5:14)? When Jonah was in the fish's belly, was he actually in *hell* (see Jonah 2:2)?

There is a second view which, as I see it, is also wrong. It is entrenched very firmly in the minds of many scholars who find it in Lexicons, Encyclopedias, etc. *This second erroneous view is the belief that the Old Testament teaches that all men go to the same place when they die, a place neither of blessedness on the one hand nor of pain on the other hand, a region of the shades, to be taken very literally.*

As I see it, the error is due to the failure to see that in many cases biblical language is to be taken figuratively, not literally. The theory in question is therefore burdened with all kinds of difficulties. If Sheol is the place to which all men go when they die, how can descent into that place be held up as *a warning* (Psalm 9:17; Proverbs 5:5; 7:27; 15:24; 23:14)? If Sheol is never a place of pain, how can Moses tell us that *God's anger burns there* (Deuteronomy 32:22)? And if the Old Testament teaches that at death everybody goes to the dreary abode of the shades, how then is it that believers faced death *with joyful expectation* (Numbers 23:10; Psalm 16:9-11; 17:15; 73:24-26)?

A third erroneous view, rather popular also in some evangelical circles, is this: Sheol is the underworld with its two divisions, one for the righteous and one for the wicked. But in the Old Testament a divided Sheol is nowhere taught. Psalm 9:17 does not say that the wicked shall be turned into a division of Sheol, but into Sheol. Proverbs 15:24 does not urge a person to avoid a compartment in Sheol, but *Sheol itself.* And we never read that at death God's children went to this or that *division* of Sheol. The idea of a Sheol with two divisions is derived from the pagan view of the underworld. Neither Sheol in the Old nor Hades in the New has that meaning.

The fourth erroneous view is that of Pastor Russell. Though, as we have pointed out, he is partly right in criticizing the rendering that occurs in the Authorized Version, he is wrong in teaching that in that Version the rendering "hell" is uniformly wrong. And he is wrong especially in his own rendering. According to Pastor Russell, and the Jehovah's Witnesses after him, Sheol means Oblivion or Non-existence. That is entirely wrong.

You can see that for yourself in noticing what happens when you substitute the word Non-existence for Sheol in such a passage as Deuteronomy 32:22. Is the fire of God's anger actually burning "unto the lowest Non-existence"? Can anybody make any sense out of that? Nor would it make sense to say that this fire is burning "unto the lowest grave."

2. What I Believe to Be the Right View

Sheol is the state or the place into which a person descends, whether literally or figuratively. As such the word has a variety of meanings, and in each separate instance of its use the context must decide what is meant.

a. At times Sheol is *the place of punishment for the wicked.* In such cases *hell* is a good rendering. See Deuteronomy 32:22; Psalm 9:17; 55:15; Proverbs 15:11, 24; etc. In such passages Sheol is the place where God's wrath burns, and to which the wicked at death *descend,* the wicked and not the righteous.

b. In other passages Sheol probably refers to *the grave,* into which indeed all men, righteous as well as wicked, *descend* (as to the body) when they die. Think of Jacob's "gray hairs" descending into Sheol, that is, into the grave (Genesis 44:29, 31; I Kings 2:6, 9).

c. In several other passages "state of death," "disembodied existence," may well be what is meant. But now note well: this state of separation between soul and body is then represented *as if* it were a place (I Samuel 2:6), equipped with gates (Isaiah 38:10). Of course, all men do indeed *descend* into that place, *conceived figuratively.* Whether you are a believer or whether you are an unbeliever, when you die, your soul and body separates; hence, in that sense, everybody goes to Sheol at death.

But the point to note is this: *in no passage either Old or New Testament is it taught that the souls of all men actually go to the same place, literally, at death.* On the contrary, the Bible consistently teaches that at death the wicked are doomed forever and the righteous (in Christ, of course) are blessed forever.

3. The Meaning of Hades in the New Testament

In the parable of the Rich Man and Lazarus (Luke 16) Hades is not the underworld with two divisions, one of them being "Abraham's bosom," the other something else. On the contrary, Hades there means *hell.* It is the place of *torments* and of *the flame* (Luke 16:23, 24). So also *hell* may well be *the correct rendering* of Hades in Matthew 11:23 and in Luke 10:15, for here Hades is sharply contrasted with *heaven;* hence, *hell,* probably to be understood in the *figurative* sense of *thorough ruin.* In Matthew 16:18 the thought may well be that not even all the demons streaming forth out of the gates of *hell* will ever be able to destroy Christ's true church. In Acts 2:27, 31 the term Hades is by many interpreted as indicating that the soul of Jesus was *not abandoned* to the state of death (disembodied existence), not left in that state. It means either that or the phrase "my soul" (according to a well-known underlying Hebrew idiom) simply means "me." Thus construed, the entire passage (Acts 2:22-31) would point to the fact that *Christ's* flesh (in contrast with *David's)* was not left to see corruption in *the grave,* but on the third day was gloriously raised. In the three Hades-passages in the book of Revelation (1:18; 6:8; 20:13, 14) Hades probably refers to the state of death. However, here again this state is represented figuratively, *as if* it were *a place* (to which Jesus has the key) or *a person* (who always follows Death, 6:8, and is at last cast into the lake of fire, 20:13, 14).

FOR DISCUSSION

A. *Based on This Chapter*

1. Why is the study of Sheol and Hades of some importance?

2. Describe and refute four erroneous views regarding the meaning of Sheol.

3. What do you regard as being the correct view as to the meaning of Sheol?

4. What rule must one follow in order to determine the meaning of Sheol in any specific passage?

5. What are the various shades of meaning of Hades in the New Testament?

B. *Further Discussion*

1. Does the term Hades ever refer to the final state of the wicked after Christ's second coming?

2. What does the American Standard Version do with the terms Sheol and Hades? Do you approve?

3. What is the main point of the parable of the Rich Man and Lazarus?

4. What wrong had the rich man committed? Had he been a murderer, thief, adulterer? If not, why was he committed to hell?

5. Was Lazarus received by the angels into Abraham's bosom because he had been poor on earth?

Chapter 18

Is There Such a Place As Purgatory?

Read Hebrews 10:11-18

1. A Sharp Contrast

The story is told that a certain devout member of the Roman Catholic Church, realizing that death was approaching, exclaimed, "O blessed purgatory!" Cardinal Gibbons calls the doctrine of purgatory "a cherished doctrine," and with respect to prayers for the souls in purgatory he states, "I cannot recall any doctrine of the Christian religion more consoling to the human heart than the article of faith which teaches the efficacy of prayers for the faithful departed. It robs death of its sting" (*The Faith Of Our Fathers*, pp. 211, 223, 224).

On the other hand, having been a member of the church of Rome for fifty years and having functioned as priest for half of that period, Father Chiniquy, the convert to Protestantism, wrote, "How long, O Lord, shall that insolent enemy of the gospel, the Church of Rome, be permitted to fatten herself upon the tears of the widow and of the orphan by means of that cruel and impious invention of paganism — purgatory?" (*Fifty Years in the Church of Rome*, p. 48).

The doctrine of purgatory: "a cherished doctrine...consoling to the human heart," or "a cruel and impious invention of paganism," what is it?

2. Rome's Doctrine of Purgatory Summarized

In the words of Cardinal Gibbons, "The Catholic Church teaches that, besides a place of eternal torments for the wicked and of everlasting rest for the righteous, there exists in the next life a middle state of temporary punishment, allotted for those who have died in venial sin, or who have not satisfied the justice of God for sins already forgiven. She also teaches us that, although the souls consigned to this intermediate state, commonly called purgatory, cannot help themselves, they may be aided by the suffrages of the faithful on earth" (*op. cit.*, p. 210).

By the Council of Trent the Roman Catholic doctrine concerning purgatory was thus defined:

"There is a purgatory, and souls there detained are helped by the prayers of the faithful, and especially by the acceptable Sacrifice of the Altar" (Session XXV).

"This holy council commands all bishops diligently to endeavor that the wholesome doctrine concerning purgatory...be believed, held, taught, and everywhere preached by Christ's faithful" (Session XXV).

With respect to the man who rejects this doctrine the same council declared, "Let him be anathema" (that is, accursed) (Session VI).

Roman Catholic doctrine includes the following elements:

a. Purgatory is the place where the souls of by far the most deceased believers suffer anguish, and are thereby gradually purified.

b. Thus these souls pay off the remainder of their debt. In purgatory they bear whatever remains to be borne of the temporal punishment for the sins which they committed while they were still on earth.

c. The duration as well as the intensity of suffering varies. Some suffer more, some less. Some are in anguish for a longer period, some for a shorter time. This depends, to some extent, on the kind of life which *these souls themselves* have lived while still on earth. It also depends, to some extent, on what *their friends on earth* are doing for them; that is, on the prayers which these friends offer for them, the indulgences which they obtain for them, and especially on the masses which they cause to be said for them.

d. The friends still living on earth must pay for these masses.

e. The pope exercises some kind of jurisdiction over purgatory. For example, it is his prerogative, by granting indulgences, to lighten the anguish of the soul in purgatory or even to terminate it.

3. Lack of Scriptural Proof

When the question is asked, "Where do I find all this in the

Bible?" the answer given by Roman Catholics, such as Cardinal Gibbons, is very revealing. After saying that this doctrine is "plainly contained in the Old Testament," he quotes *one* passage, and that passage is taken from a book which by Protestants is rightfully considered as *apocryphal*. The quotation is from II Maccabees "with its palpable exaggerations and its frequent moralizings" (Bruce M. Metzger, *An Introduction To The Apocrypha*, p. 146). The passage is 12:43-45. But even that passage does not prove the Roman Catholic doctrine, for it speaks about prayer for soldiers who had died in the *mortal* (not *venial*) sin of idolatry.

Gibbons also refers to *two* New Testament passages. The first is Matthew 12:32, which tells us that the sin against the Holy Spirit will not be forgiven either in this age or in the age to come. Of course, this means that the sin indicated will *never* be forgiven. It does not mean that some sins will be forgiven in the age to come. But even if it meant that, it still would be of no help whatever to the Roman Catholic doctrine, for the age to come is that which follows Christ's second coming, when, according to Roman Catholic doctrine, purgatory will have ceased to exist.

The second passage is I Corinthians 3:12-15. I shall not take the time to offer a detailed exegesis of that passage. The following suffices to show that it lends no support to any doctrine of purgatory. The fire which reveals and tests *the works* of men is certainly not the literal fire which according to Roman Catholic doctrine cleanses *their souls*. Again, according to I Corinthians 3:15 some men are saved *"so as* through fire," not at all "through fire." And lastly, the main reference of this scriptural passage is not to the intermediate state but to that which will happen on "the day," that is, the judgment day, when, as has already been indicated, purgatory will be a thing of the past.

Other Roman Catholic authors have tried to find support for this doctrine in such passages as Isaiah 4:4; Micah 7:8; Zechariah 9:11; Malachi 3:2, 3; Matthew 5:22, 25, 26; and Revelation 21:27. But a mere look at these passages immediately indicates that they have nothing to do with purgatory.

4. Rome's Doctrine of Purgatory a Downright Heresy

a. *It is in conflict with sound Theology and Anthropology* (Scripture's doctrine concerning God and man). While Scripture everywhere stresses the fact that *man cannot save himself* (Romans 3:21-27; 7:14-25; 8:3) and that basically *salvation is God's work* (Psalm 32:1, 2; Romans 7:24, 25; Ephesians 2:8-10; Titus 3:4-7; I Peter 1:19), the doctrine of purgatory shifts the emphasis away from God and toward man. According to Rome's teaching it is definitely *man* who, to a certain extent, pays the bill, endures the temporal punishment due to his sins, earns salvation. In fact, some men, according to this doctrine, are able in this present life to perform more than their share of good works. The merits of their "works of supererogation" are applied to the souls in purgatory! *Such a doctrine fails completely to fathom the depth of man's fall, and deprives God of the honor due to him* (Romans 11:36).

b. *It is in conflict with sound Christology* (Scripture's doctrine concerning Christ). According to the Bible "Jesus paid it all." It was he who obtained for his people eternal redemption (Hebrews 9:12) by the sacrifice of himself (Hebrews 9:26). Moreover, it was by means of his *one* offering that he perfected forever those who are sanctified (Hebrews 10:14). "The blood of Jesus Christ his Son cleanses us from *all* sin" (I John 1:7; see also Hebrews 5:9; Revelation 1:5). This biblical teaching leaves no room whatever for the Roman Catholic doctrine of purgatory.

c. *It is in conflict with sound Soteriology* (Scripture's doctrine concerning salvation). According to the Bible a man is *justified* by faith in Christ's merits (Romans 5:1), and not in any sense by his own merits. He is *sanctified* by the Holy Spirit (II Thessalonians 2:13) and not by the fabulous fires of purgatory.

d. *It is in conflict with sound Ecclesiology* (Scripture's doctrine concerning the church and the sacraments). What a contrast between the church as pictured by Paul in Ephesians 5:25-27 — "glorious, without spot or wrinkle or any such thing, holy and without blemish" — and an institution which has left the impression upon many that it is altogether too money-minded!

e. *It is in conflict with sound Eschatology* (Scripture's doctrine concerning the last things). According to Scripture there is a hell for the wicked, a heaven for God's children. See this for yourself by examining Psalm I; Psalm 73; Daniel 12:2; Matthew 7:13, 14; 7:24-27; 25:1-13, 31-46; John 3:16; II Thessalonians 1:8-10; Revelation 20:11-15; 22:14, 15. *There is no purgatory.*

FOR DISCUSSION

A. *Based on This Chapter*

1. In what terms do some Roman Catholics praise the doctrine of purgatory?

2. How do others, with long experience in the church of Rome, condemn it?

3. Summarize Rome's doctrine of purgatory.

4. Show that the passages of the Bible to which Rome appeals fail to prove this doctrine.

5. Prove that this doctrine is a downright heresy.

B. *Further Discussion*

1. Where did Rome get its doctrine of purgatory?

2. Is it a very comforting doctrine? Is it fair to the poor?

3. How does Rome distinguish between that which Christ did to save us from sin and that which we ourselves must do?

4. What was Luther's attitude toward the doctrine of purgatory?

5. How would you try to convince a Roman Catholic that he should turn away from this glaring error?

Chapter 19

Will There Be Perfect Equality in the Hereafter or Will There Be Degrees of Weal and Woe?

Read Matthew 25:14-30

1. The Urge to Equalize

"Soak the rich and raise the living standard of the poor." "Redistribute wealth so that everyone will have an equal portion." Such are the slogans we hear on every side. Many people seem to believe that if only this wonderful ideal could be reached, all problems would be solved and everyone would be happy ever after.

More thorough investigation usually reveals the fact that the "equality" which many confess to be seeking is a rather variable and subjective commodity. To be sure, Mr. Brown wants to have a share of Mr. Jones's wealth, for Jones is richer than Brown. But Mr. Brown is not at all anxious to share *his own* wealth with poorer Mr. Black. Besides, it stands to reason that if the rich were suddenly deprived of their work-creating capital, the result would not be prosperity for all but poverty for all. This does not mean that anyone should be indifferent to the lot of the poor. Far from it. Indifference in word and deed would be definitely un-Christian. Moreover, there is no excuse for "hoarding." But perfect equality to be reached by share-the-wealth programs is an ideal which is both impractical and unbiblical (Proverbs 6:6-11; 24:30-34).

2. Equality in Heaven?

"But surely in heaven we shall all be equal," says someone. I answer, Yes, in the sense that all who enter there will have been sinners who are then in the state of having been "saved by grace."

All, moreover, will owe their salvation *equally* to the sovereign love of God. And the goal for all will be *the same:* to glorify God and enjoy him forever. Nevertheless, there will be inequalities, differences, *degrees* of weal (and in hell degrees of woe). In a previous chapter it has been shown that in all probability there is progress, development even in heaven, so that the redeemed will resemble the gradually opening petals of a flower. At first such a flower has room for only a few dewdrops, but the more it opens up, the greater its capacity becomes. Nevertheless even so the blue forget-me-not will never sparkle with as many dewdrops as will the tulip waving its stately head in the next garden bed. Forget-me-nots will never be tulips nor sunflowers. Though there is growth and development for every species of flowers, yet from the very beginning there is difference in capacity.

Scripture teaches this doctrine of "degrees of glory." When Jesus comes to reward his servants, one of these faithful ones will in the end have *ten* talents (in fact, *eleven,* Matthew 25:28), another *four* talents. There will be those in the life hereafter who will receive a *reward* which others, though saved, will not receive, that is, not in equal measure (I Corinthians 3:10-15). Everyone will be judged "according to his works." Are there not also differences among the angels? Is *every* angel an archangel?

3. If Not Equal, What Determines the Difference?

First, the difference is determined by the degree of faithfulness shown while the redeemed were still living on earth. That is a very important point. But it is not everything, as also the Parable of the Talents shows. At the very outset, to one servant five talents were entrusted, to another only two. It is not for us to quarrel with the manner in which God, according to his good and sovereign will, distributes his gifts. And if one answers, "Yes, but even in this parable the talents were entrusted *according to the ability of each servant,*" the answer is, "And who was the Author of this ability?" Read I Corinthians 4:7, "What hast thou that thou hast not received?" For us it should be sufficient to know that all of the redeemed will be thoroughly satisfied; in fact, they will say, "The half was not told me."

4. Equality in Hell?

Even in hell there are degrees of difference. Not all suffer alike. For some the punishment will be "more tolerable" than for others. See Matthew 11:22, 24). This will be made clear as we study the next chapter.

FOR DISCUSSION

A. *Based on This Chapter*

1. Discuss "the urge to equalize."
2. In which sense will there be equality in heaven?
3. In which sense will there not be equality?
4. What determines the difference in degrees of glory?
5. Are there degrees of punishment in hell?

B. *Further Discussion*

1. Would you appeal to John 14:2 to prove that there are degrees of glory in heaven?
2. Does Paul teach degrees of glory in I Corinthians 15:41?
3. Do degrees of glory imply differences in tasks?
4. Study the rule laid down in Matthew 25:29. Is that rule fair?
5. What is the practical lesson contained in the Parable of the Talents? In which way does this parable differ from that of the Pounds (Luke 19:11-27)?

Chapter 20

Are Those Who Never Heard the Gospel Saved?

Read Amos 3:1, 2; Luke 12:47, 48

1. The Objector States: "The Doctrine of Hell Is a Cruel Doctrine, for It Teaches That God Casts into the Depths of Hell Countless Innocent Pagans Who Have Never Heard the Gospel."

Answer

a. "Into *the depths* of hell"? The objector is forgetting that there are degrees of punishment in hell. According to Leviticus 26:28 those who, being covenant children, refuse to walk in the covenant way, will be punished "seven times" for their sins. Amos 3:2 teaches that woeful judgments will be visited upon Israel because, though specially privileged, it has nevertheless turned its back upon Jehovah. Luke 12:47, 48 indicates that those who, having known the way, have not walked in it, will be severely lashed, while those who have not known the way and have deserved a beating will receive much lighter punishment. Romans 2:12-16 proves that while those who have sinned without the law will perish without the law, those who have sinned under the law will be judged by the law. And Hebrews 10:29 speaks of sorer punishment for those who have trodden under foot the Son of God than for those who have set at nought the law of Moses. Cf. Matthew 11:20-24; Luke 10:12-15; 11:31, 32.

The fact that the degree of light which a person has received will make a difference is the teaching of Scripture throughout. This does not mean that those who sinned in a state of relative ignorance are completely without guilt. But it does mean that a just God does not leave out of account the privileges and opportunities which a person has enjoyed, or the lack of these advantages. See also Luke 23:34; Acts 3:17; and I Timothy 1:13.

Hence, when anyone states that God casts *"into the lowest hell"* those who have lived and died in the blindness of heathendom, he is saying something that is contrary to Scripture. Not the blind heathen but "the sons of the kingdom" are the ones who, because of their disobedience, will be cast into *outer* darkness (Matthew 8:12).

b. *"innocent* pagans"? The objector forgets that even these blind heathen are by no means innocent. Below are some samples of wickedness that were reliably reported to me by missionaries. Note that word *missionaries.* It implies that many of the people among whom they performed their labors were no longer *completely* in darkness. Therefore, if even among *them* conditions were as reported, how much more so among those entirely unreached?

dishonesty: "I am sorry that I cannot come to the meeting. You see, my mother-in-law died, and I must attend the funeral." Fact subsequently discovered: the mother-in-law had died and had been buried years ago. The same missionary related to me scores of similar instances of dishonesty, some of them almost unbelievable.

cruelty: "Ashamed of myself? Why should I be? She disobeyed me, therefore I punish her." The missionary found this man's wife hanging headdown from the branch of a tree. Slavery, torture, cannibalism, infanticide, sodomy, and many other crimes abound among the so-called "innocent" heathen. Basic to all is the fact that their *state* is that of condemnation in Adam (Romans 5:12, 17, 18). *By nature* all men are children of wrath, sold under sin, lying in the evil one (Ephesians 2:3; Romans 7:14; I John 5:19).

rejecting God: "I hate your God." Thus spoke this heathen when for the first time he heard the voice of God's messenger describing to him the God of justice and of love, as revealed in Holy Writ. And does not Romans 1:18-32 teach that the heathen *rebelliously suppress and pervert* the truth? Be sure to read that entire paragraph—verses 18-32—in order to be cured of any notion that the Gentiles are "innocent."

2. The Objector Continues: "Not All the Heathen Are Wicked. There Are Gentiles Who, Though They Have Not the Law, Do by Nature the Things of the Law (Romans 2:14). Will Not These Be Saved Even Though They Never Heard the Gospel?"

Answer

It is true, indeed, that the glimmerings of natural light whereby man shows some regard for virtue and for good outward behavior are far more evident in some than in others. But these glimmerings are insufficient to bring even the best Gentile to a saving knowledge of God and to true conversion. God sees not only the outward deed but also the heart of man. In his heart man is proud of his good deeds. Thus he shows that he is not even able to use aright the light which he has received. All his "righteousnesses" are like a polluted garment. It is true, to be sure, that some heathen are far more wicked than others. For these "others" hell's punishment will be far lighter. But *salvation* is based on grace, not on works. If anyone doubts the fact that faith in Jesus Christ is the only way to salvation, let him study the following passages: John 3:16; 5:12; 14:6; 15:5; Acts 4:12; Romans 3:23, and I Corinthians 3:11. Acts 16:14 and Romans 10:12-15 show how man normally arrives at faith in Christ.

3. The Objector Presents a Final Objection: "If Salvation Depends on Hearing the Gospel, Why Does Not God Cause Everybody to Hear It?"

Answer

One might add, And why does not God in his almighty providence grant riches, health, and happiness to everybody? Says Dr. H. Bavinck, "Round about us we observe so many facts which seem to be unreasonable, so...many unaccountable calamities, such an uneven and inexplicable distribution of destiny, and such an enormous contrast between the extremes of joy and sorrow, that any one reflecting on these things is forced to choose between viewing this universe as if it were governed by the blind will of an unbenign deity as is done by pessimism, or, upon the basis of Scripture and by faith, resting on the absolute and sovereign, yet — however incomprehensible — wise and holy will of

him who will one day cause the full light of heaven
upon these mysteries of life" (*The Doctrine Of God, English
translation*, p. 396). See Romans 9:20; then also Job 11:7 and
Isaiah 55:8, 9. One fact is certain: man lost in Adam, and adding
to his sin every day, has no inherent right either to salvation
or to hearing the way of salvation. If he hears it, that is grace.
The plight of the heathen should lead not to a criticism of God
but to unabating zeal to obey his command to proclaim the
gospel to all the nations. The rule surely is that without the
saving knowledge of Christ the Gentiles *perish* (Romans 1:32;
2:12; Revelation 21:8). *Rescue the perishing!* (John 3:16).

FOR DISCUSSION

A. *Based on This Chapter*

1. What is the objector's first argument?
2. How do you answer it?
3. What is his second argument?
4. How do you answer that?
5. What is his third argument, and how do you answer that?

B. *Further Discussion*

1. Discuss the statement, "The heathen are hungry for the gospel."
2. Do you believe that it is impossible for any adult heathen to be
saved unless he hears the gospel preached? Cannot God reveal the gospel
to him in a dream or in a vision or perhaps even in some other way?
What about those who are so very seriously retarded mentally that even
if they heard the gospel it would not benefit them?
3. Do you believe that Socrates and Plato were saved?
4. Is it right to attempt a "theodicy"?
5. What relation has this chapter to the urgency of doing mission-
work? How can we bind this great cause upon the hearts of our children
and young people?

Chapter 21

Are All Those Who Died in Infancy Saved?

Read Jonah 4:6-11; I Corinthians 7:14

1. The Importance of This Subject

Until recently a very high percentage of humans never attained to maturity. In fact, ever so many died in infancy. Of late this tragic situation has taken a turn for the better. Concerted efforts are being put forth to counteract the high rate of infant mortality and to improve the health of the nations. Think of what is being done by the World Health Organization (W.H.O.), an agency of the Economic and Social Council of the United Nations, and by other agencies all over the world. Even so the goal is not yet in sight.

The question naturally arises, Where are the souls of all these millions upon millions who died in infancy? Where, indeed, are those who constitute a surprisingly large proportion of the sum-total of all those who at one time or another lived upon this earth, be it only for a few years, months, weeks, days, hours, or even minutes or seconds? Must we believe that by far the most of them are in some sense experiencing the agonies of everlasting perdition?

2. Wrong Approaches

First, there is what may be called the prevailing view in the Roman Catholic Church. It amounts to this: *all unbaptized children are lost,* in the sense that when they die they enter the *Limbus Infantum* (or *Infantium*), a place on the outskirts of hell. Their suffering here is negative rather than positive. They suffer the lack of "beatific vision."

Now this approach, while containing indeed an element of truth (inasmuch as it rightly recognizes the fact that responsibility varies with opportunity), is wrong on two counts: a. Scripture nowhere ascribes such importance to the omission of the rite of baptism; b. it also nowhere teaches the existence of a *Limbus Infantum.*

Over against this is the position of those who hold that all babies are "innocent." According to this view, "original sin," if it can be spoken of at all, is not punishable apart from actual transgression. Since little children are not capable of actual trangression but are innocent, *all are saved* if they die in infancy. This or something akin to it is the position of many evangelical Protestants today. As brothers in Christ we love these people, but we do not believe that Scripture endorses this reason for their position. Infants, too, are guilty in Adam. Moreover, they are not innocent (see Job 14:4; Psalm 51:5; Romans 5:12, 18, 19; I Corinthians 15:22; and Ephesians 2:3). If they are going to be saved at all, this salvation will have to be granted on the basis not of their innocence but of the application of Christ's merits to them.

3. The Official Position of the Presbyterian Church U.S.A.

The Westminster Confession does not give a clear answer to the question whether all those who die in infancy are saved. In fact, it rather leaves room for the opinion that some might not be elect and saved. See this for yourself. It states, "Elect infants, dying in infancy, are regenerated and saved by Christ through the Spirit, who worketh when and where and how he pleaseth" (Chapter X, Section III). In the year 1903 the Presbyterian Church U.S.A. has, however, "interpreted" this article so that today one knows exactly where this denomination now stands with respect to that issue. It adopted the following Declaratory Statement:

"The Presbyterian Church in the United States of America does authoritatively declare as follows...With reference to Chapter X, Section III, of the Confession of Faith, that it is not regarded as teaching that any who die in infancy are lost. We believe that all dying in infancy are included in the election of grace, and are regenerated and saved by Christ through the Spirit, who works when and where and how he pleases."

4. Quotations from the Works of Reformed Theologians

"All who die in infancy are saved. This is inferred from what the Bible teaches of the analogy between Adam and Christ (Romans 5:18, 19).... The Scriptures nowhere exclude any class of infants, baptized or unbaptized, born in Christian or in heathen lands, of believing or unbelieving parents, from the benefits of redemption in Christ" (Charles Hodge, *Systematic Theology*, Vol. I, p. 26).

"Their destiny is determined irrespective of their choice, by an unconditional decree of God, suspended for its execution on no act of their own; and their salvation is wrought by an unconditional application of the grace of Christ to their souls, through the immediate and irresistible operation of the Holy Spirit prior to and apart from any action of their own proper wills.... This is but to say that they are unconditionally predestinated to salvation from the foundation of the world" (B. B. Warfield, *Two Studies in the History of Doctrine*, p. 230).

"Most Calvinistic theologians have held that those who die in infancy are saved....Certainly there is nothing in the Calvinistic system which would prevent us from believing this; and until it is proven that God could not predestinate to eternal life all those whom he is pleased to call in infancy we may be permitted to hold this view" (L. Boettner, *The Reformed Doctrine of Predestination*, pp. 143, 144.

Nevertheless, not all Reformed theologians speak so positively. Some bring out more clearly the difference, as they see it, between infants *of believers* and *all other* infants. "The children of the covenant, baptized or unbaptized, when they die enter heaven; with respect to the destiny of the others so little has been revealed to us that the best thing we can do is to refrain from any positive judgment" (H. Bavinck, *Gereformeerde Dogmatiek*, third edition, Vol. IV, p. 711, my translation).

Similarly, L. Berkhof, while in full agreement with the Canons of Dort regarding the salvation of children *of godly parents* whom it pleases God to call out of this life in their infancy, states with respect to *the others*, "There is no Scripture evidence on which we can base the hope that...Gentile children that have not yet come to years of discretion will be saved"(*Systematic Theology*, pp. 638, 693).

5. Scriptural Teaching

a. If those who die in their infancy are saved, it is not on the basis of their innocence but on the basis of the sovereign grace of God in Christ applied to them (see under point 2 above).

b. The fact that the heart of God is concerned not only with the children of believers but also with those of unbelievers, even with those "who cannot discern between their right hand and their left" is clearly taught in Jonah 4:11.

c. "God's tender mercies are over all his works," and "God is love" (Psalm 145:9; I John 4:8). One is therefore permitted to agree with the beautiful lines:

> "For the love of God is broader
> Than the measure of man's mind
> And the heart of the Eternal
> Is most wonderfully kind."
> —F. W. Faber, 1854

d. Infants have not sinned in any way similar to the adults who have rejected the preaching of the gospel and/or have sinned grossly against the voice of conscience.

e. Scripture nowhere explicitly teaches that all unbelievers' children who died in infancy are saved. Though on the basis of b, c, and d a person may feel strongly inclined to accept the position that all of these are saved, he can never say that Scripture positively and in so many words declares this to be true.

f. God has given *to believers and their seed* the promise found in Genesis 17:7 and Acts 2:38, 39. Cf. also I Corinthians 7:14. Hence, the Canons of Dort declare, "Since we are to judge of the will of God from his Word, which testifies that the children of believers are holy, not by nature, but by virtue of the covenant of grace, in which they together with their parents are comprehended, godly parents ought not to doubt the election and salvation of their children whom it pleases God to call out of this life in their infancy" (I, article 17).

FOR DISCUSSION

A. *Based on This Chapter*

1. Why is this subject important?

2. Describe two wrong approaches.

3. What is the official position of the Presbyterian Church U.S.A.?

4. What was the position of Hodge and Warfield? Of Bavinck and Berkhof?

5. What is the Scriptural teaching with respect to this subject?

B. *Further Discussion*

1. Would you appeal to I Kings 14:13 to prove that some unbelievers' children who die in infancy *are saved*? To Zechariah 8:5? To Mark 10:14?

2. Do you agree with Hodge's exegesis of Romans 5:18, 19?

3. Would you appeal to Numbers 16:31-33 (or similar passages) to prove that some unbelievers' children who die in infancy *are lost*?

4. What was the view of Luther with respect to this subject? Of Zwingli? Of Calvin?

5. "Satan gets the greatest number." True or false? What is meant by the age of accountability? When does a child arrive at that age? Is it important that the matter of accountability be impressed on the heart of the growing child?

Chapter 22

Will Those Who Died Unsaved Have a Chance to Be Saved Afterward?

Read Matthew 25:1-13

1. The Exact Question

There are two misconceptions of which we should free our minds immediately. On the one hand, there are the people who belong to this or that sect. These will sometimes confuse their victims by telling them that it is *not* true that they believe in *"second* probation" (a *second* trial-period or *second* chance). Their argument is this: "The heathen, and many others besides, never really had a chance. Hence, an opportunity to be saved after death is really not a *second* probation. It is their *first* chance." Therefore, in the wording of the question as you find it above this chapter I have purposely avoided the word "second."

There is also an error (of omission, I suppose) of which even some excellent works on doctrine are guilty. They write about this entire matter *as if it had reference only to "the intermediate state"* (the time between the moment when the person dies and the moment when he is raised from the dead). But that is not entirely true. To be sure, in the course of the history of doctrine there have arisen many individuals and sects that have confined "the after-death-opportunity-to-be-saved" to the intermediate state, but that does not hold with respect to all of them. The Russellites, for example, believe that those who have died have gone "out of existence," but *will be recreated.* They will appear *at the end of history* with the same thoughts in their brains and the very same words on their tongues that were there at the moment of dissolution. Then (in the millennium) will come the chance to be saved.

But whether a sect or a person believes in a chance to be

saved during the intermediate state or at the time of the resurrection, in either case the belief is that *after death* (be it *shortly*
afterward or *long* afterward) there will still be such an opportunity to be saved.

2. The Arguments of Those Who Accept a Future Probation

These arguments are not the same for every group. Some
stress this, others that, depending on the particular future-
probation theory which they hold. All stress the idea that the
fairness of God demands that he give men this chance to be
saved after death. Some try to show that to be damned one
must have wilfully rejected the offer of salvation. Those who
believe that a chance to be saved will be given to men (at least
to *some* of them) in the intermediate state generally appeal to
I Peter 3:18, 19 and I Peter 4:6, which passages are then interpreted to mean that Christ in the period between his death and
resurrection went to the underworld and there extended the
invitation unto salvation to the spirits of the lost. And finally,
those who connect the chance to be saved with the resurrection
at the close of history fantastically apply "Scripture-passages
regarding Israel's restoration" to the future restoration and
probation of men in general. They usually add that the resurrection of all these people (who, by the way, had already gone
"out of existence") will afford them a chance to make good
use of their past experience. This "past experience will thus
serve as a deterrent on the one hand and a spur to better things
on the other." Should they, however, choose to live in sin
their punishment will consist in *annihilation*.

3. Scriptural Proof That This Doctrine Is False

a. Scripture teaches that it is not up to us to tell God what
is fair and what is not fair. As I wrote previously: "Man lost
in Adam, and adding to his sin every day, has no inherent right
either to salvation or to hearing the way of salvation." See
also Daniel 4:35 and Romans 9:20.

b. It is not true that in order to be damned man must have
rejected the offer of salvation (Romans 1:32; 2:12; Revelation
21:8).

c. The interpretation of I Peter 3:18, 19 offered by the future probationists is indeed "a very precarious exegesis of a most difficult passage in Peter's Epistle" (A. T. Robertson, *Word Pictures,* Vol. VI, p. 117). Even if that interpretation were correct, it still would not suffice to prove the theory unless it be supposed that in the realm of "the wicked dead" missionary activity *is continually going on.* It is also difficult to see why, passing by multitudes of other lost souls, Christ would have selected for his mission work in the underworld exactly those souls (namely, of the antediluvians) who while still in the flesh had had every opportunity to repent (Genesis 6:3; Hebrews 11:7). As to I Peter 4:6, the context (see verse 5) clearly indicates that here "the dead" to whom the gospel is preached are those who when Jesus comes to judge will already have died. The text does not mean that the gospel is preached to men while they are in the state of death (the intermediate state).

d. The jump from Israel's restoration to future probation for men in general is so big and so exegetically unsound that no further comment is necessary.

e. Scripture teaches that the state of unbelievers after death is a fixed state. For the rich man in the parable of Luke 16:19-31 there is clearly no further opportunity to be saved. The wicked are kept under punishment until the day of the final judgment (II Peter 2:4, 9). The blackness of darkness is reserved for them, and this *forever* (Jude 13).

f. When once the Bridegroom arrives, those who "are ready" enter. For the others the door will be *shut* (Matthew 25:10-13). This exclusion lasts *forevermore* (Matthew 25:46). The resurrection is unto *life* or unto *damnation, not unto probation* (John 5:28, 29). The risen ones are judged according to that which they have done not in the intermediate state but while still in the flesh (Matthew 7:22, 23; 10:32, 33; 25:34-46; Luke 12:47, 48; II Corinthians 5:9, 10; Galatians 6:7, 8; II Thessalonians 1:8, 9).

g. After death comes not probation but judgment (Hebrews 9:27).

h. Scripture admonishes men that the day of salvation is *now,* not at some future date, whether that date be in the intermediate state or at the close of history (Psalm 95:7, 8; II Corinthians 6:2).

FOR DISCUSSION

A. *Based on This Chapter*

1. Do all those who believe in a future probation refer this to the intermediate state?

2. What are the arguments of those who, in one form or another, accept the doctrine of a chance to be saved for those who have already died?

3. Is it up to us to tell God what is fair and what is not fair? Prove your answer by quoting Scripture.

4. Is it true that in order to be damned a man must have rejected the offer of salvation?

5. What are some of the other arguments showing that according to Scripture those who were not saved when they died have no chance to be saved afterward?

B. *Further Discussion*

1. How do *you* interpret I Peter 3:18, 19?

2. What effect does the doctrine of probation after death have on doing effective mission work?

3. Can you tell the story of Pastor Russell's life?

4. What are the main tenets of Russellism? What is the best way to deal with Russellism?

5. What is the main lesson of the parable of the Five Wise and the Five Foolish Virgins?

General Eschatology

Chapter 23

Which Group Has the Right Attitude, the Men of Laodicea, of Thessalonica, or of Smyrna?

Read Revelation 3:14-22;
II Thessalonians 2:1, 2; 3:6-12
Revelation 2:8-11

1. The Lord Is at Hand

One day, long ago, Paul told the Thessalonians that their Lord would return "as a thief in the night" (I Thessalonians 5:2).

A little later the churches of Asia Minor were told that his coming would be "with the clouds," and that the time was "at hand" (Revelation 1:3, 7).

Ever since the days of Christ's incarnation the church has been living in "the last days." Surely if "the signs of the times" (Matthew 16:3) were in evidence during our Lord's sojourn on earth, so that Pharisees and Sadducees were chided for their failure to observe them, they must be in evidence now.

But in their attitude toward these signs people differ. There is, for example, the attitude of the men of Laodicea. There is also the attitude of *some* people in Thessalonica. And finally, there is the attitude of the church at Smyrna.

2. The Men of Laodicea

Their attitude was that of *lukewarmness*. They were too busy with earthly matters to bother about matters pertaining to the spiritual realm (cf. Luke 17:26-32). Whenever anyone spoke about the blessed hope, their hearts did not begin to throb with joy, neither did their souls begin to be consumed with longing, with joyful anticipation. Their eyes did not attempt to pierce the clouds, neither did they strain their ears to hear the

111

joyful sounds of the angel's trumpet. When anyone held out to them the prospect of complete deliverance from sin and the curse, this message of cheer did not produce in them the response of gratitude and praise. In fact, they were not deeply concerned with their own sinfulness. *They* had arrived!

Now the Lord was thoroughly disgusted with them and with their attitude of lukewarmness. He was about to spew them out of his mouth. He tells them that far from being the rich people they imagined themselves to be, they were in reality very poor. Far from being fortunate, they were to be pitied.

Yet, even though he abhors their lack of interest in spiritual matters, he thus earnestly admonishes them, "As many as I love, I reprove and chasten: be zealous therefore and repent. Behold I stand at the door and knock. If any one hears my voice and opens the door, I will come in to him and eat with him, and he with me" (Revelation 3:19, 20).

Indifference to spiritual matters, the spirit of lukewarmness with respect to the signs of the times, marks many people even today. To them too the Lord addresses his earnest admonition to repent.

3. Some People in Thessalonica

On the whole the church at Thessalonica was prospering spiritually. But this could not be said of *all* the members. On *some* people Paul's wonderful teaching about Christ's glorious return was having the wrong effect. *Their* attitude was that of *nervousness*. They were becoming restless and excited, so much so that they began to behave like ships that have become the victim of winds and waves and are being tossed hither and thither. They would even leave their workshops, for why should they gather earthly wealth when heavenly treasures were just around the corner? In case of pressing need the church better provide for them! Eschatology was all they cared about.

These people had to be set straight in their thinking and their disorderly conduct had to be sternly reproved.

Today too there are many excited people who speculate about the future while they neglect their present duty. They are sensationalists. They adore any roving lecturer on prophetic topics, particularly if he be willing to tell them that "according to prophecy" there is going to be such and such a war, that such and such a nation will win it, and that Christ will return at this or that specific date. The *nervousness* of such 'Thessalonians" is almost as bad as the *lukewarmness* of the Laodiceans. They should remember what Paul wrote to the Philippians: "The Lord is at hand. In nothing be anxious" (Philippians 4:5, 6).

4. The Smyrniots

The only proper attitude was that of the church at Symrna. Not *lukewarmness* nor *nervousness* but *faithfulness* characterized them. Though they experienced poverty and tribulation and though they had to endure fierce opposition from the side of those who while calling themselves the synagogue of God were in reality the synagogue of Satan, they remained loyal to their Lord and Savior Jesus Christ. Hence, though poor in material possessions they were spiritually rich. The devil will indeed cast some of them into prison and they must pass through a brief trial-period for their own further sanctification, but the crown of life awaits them. Let them persevere in their loyalty even though it costs them their lives. No one less than the Lord himself will give them their crown.

The Smyrniots, like *the better element* in the church at Thessalonica, were "awaiting God's Son out of the heavens" (I Thessalonians 1:10). While they were fully alert with respect to things to come, they at the same time attended to their spiritual duties in the here and now with such devotion that should the Bridegroom come suddenly they would be ready at any time to receive him.

Also for our own day and age this is the only proper attitude. Many things are happening which show that the coming of our Lord is approaching. With *the mind* we should make a study of these things, always in the light of Scripture. And as to *the heart*, Luke 21:28 shows the right approach, "But when these things begin to take place, look up and lift up your heads, because your redemption is drawing near."

5. Brief Summary of the Discussion Regarding the Signs

A. *The Two Preliminary Signs:*

1. The First Preliminary Sign: The Gospel Age, that is,

the preaching of the Gospel to the Whole World. This Coincides with The Millennium on Earth, that is, The Binding of Satan.

2. The Second Preliminary Sign: Satan's Little Season. Under this Heading Belong the Following:

a. The Great Apostasy

b. The Great Tribulation

c. The Reign of Antichrist

d. Concurrent Signs

B. *The One Great Final Sign:* The Appearance of the Son of Man upon Clouds of Glory with Accompanying Convulsions in the Realm of Nature.

C. *The Question with Respect to the Establishment of the State of Israel and with Respect to Israel's Conversion.* By Many Earnest Believers These Too Are Regarded As Signs of Christ's Return.

D. *The Millennium.* Since according to Revelation 20 the Millennium *precedes* The Second Coming, the logical place to discuss it would seem to be *before* the Section on The Second Coming. Also (see under A 1 above) The Gospel Age coincides with The Millennium on Earth; hence, is one of the two Preliminary Signs. But the Millennium also has its heavenly aspect. There is also The Millennium in Heaven or Reign of the Saints (that is, of their Souls). This cannot very well be a Sign for those who are still on earth. Hence, I have placed the subject of The Millennium *at the close* of the entire Section.

FOR DISCUSSION

A. *Based on This Chapter*

1. Mention the three attitudes with respect to the signs of the times.
2. Describe the men of Laodicea and their attitude.
3. Describe the attitude of some people in Thessalonica.
4. Describe the Smyrniots and their attitude.
5. Give the Summary of the discussion regarding the signs.

B. *Further Discussion*

1. What do the following passages have in common in their teaching about the Lord's return: Matthew 24:48; Hebrews 10:37; Revelation 22:7; implied also in Matthew 24:42; 25:13; Revelation 16:15?

2. Does the nearness of Christ's coming imply that it is immediately at hand?

3. Did Jesus know and teach that some time would elapse before his return? See Matthew 25:5; 25:19.

4. Did Paul know that some time would elapse before Christ's return? See II Thessalonians 2:2. Did Peter know this? See II Peter 3:3-9.

5. When our Lord refers to his *coming,* does this always refer to his eschatological coming (that is, his coming at the close of the present dispensation)? Prove your answer.

Chapter 24

The First Preliminary Sign: The Gospel Age.
What Does It Mean?

Read Matthew 24:14; Ephesians 2:11-20

1. The Setting

It is Tuesday of Passion Week. Jesus and his disciples are in the act of leaving the courts of the temple (Matthew 24:1). The disciples begin to call Christ's attention to the grandeur of the sacred edifice: "Teacher, behold, what manner of stones and what manner of buildings" (Mark 13:1). Jesus then makes the astounding prediction that this temple will be totally destroyed (Matthew 24:2).

A while later Jesus with his disciples is sitting on the mount of Olives. Across the valley they see that beautiful temple. And to think that it is going to be completely destroyed! Peter, James, John, and Andrew ask Jesus, "Tell us, when shall these things be, and what shall be the sign of thy coming and of the end of the world?" (Matthew 24:3). Note that in their thinking *Jerusalem's fall* means *the end of the world*. In this they were wrong *to some extent*. Jerusalem's fall would not immediately *usher in* the end of the world, though it would, indeed, *typify* the end of the world.

Jesus now proceeds to correct their error. He tells them that such things as the coming of false prophets, wars and rumors of wars, etc., are but *"the beginning* of travail." Moreover, he is not *immediately* and in the first instance thinking of *the end of the world* but of *the end of Jerusalem and its temple*. That this is true is very clear from the explanation given in Luke's Gospel:

"And when ye shall hear of wars and tumults, be not terrified: for these must needs come to pass first; but the end is not immediately. Then said he unto them, Nation shall arise against

116

nation, and kingdom against kingdom; and there shall be earth-quakes, and in divers places famines and pestilences; and there shall be terrors and great signs from heaven.... But when ye see *Jerusalem* (italics mine) compassed with armies, then know that her desolation is at hand" (Luke 21:9-20).

Jesus is saying, therefore, that wars and rumors of wars, famines and earthquakes, etc., though signs, will not be the signs of the *immediate* end of Jerusalem, but that the actual siege of Jerusalem by foreign armies will be that sign.

2. The Sign Itself

The disciples had asked, "Tell us, when shall these things be, and what shall be the sign of thy coming, and of the end of the world?" Jesus had answered the first part of the question. Then he proceeded to answer the second part. See verses 14 and 21. What, then, would be the sign of *Christ's coming* and of the end of *the world?* The Lord now shows that his second coming will be preceded by two great preliminary signs: a. *"the preaching of the gospel in the whole world* for a testimony to all the nations," and b. *"great tribulation* such as has not been from the beginning of the world until now, no, nor ever shall be." Hence, we know definitely that Jesus cannot return until these two predictions have been fulfilled.

Now as to the preaching of the gospel to all the nations, this is not a promise that "every person will have a chance to be saved." Jesus is saying that the world's nations shall have the opportunity at one time or another during the course of history to hear the gospel. This gospel-proclamation, moreover, will be *a testimony:* its acceptance or its rejection will be decisive. There is no promise here of any second chance: there will not be two gospel-ages, one now and the other by and by, *after* the Lord's return. What a nation does with its great opportunity in the here and now will have *final* results. This *Gospel Age* is *The Millennium on Earth.* See Chapter 33.

The fact which Jesus here states is of tremendous significance. To be sure, even during the old dispensation it had been revealed that one day the gospel of salvation would be proclaimed to the nations of the world. To Abraham God had given the promise, "In thee shall all the families of the earth be blessed" (Genesis

12:3). The Psalmist had described the One who would "have dominion also from sea to sea, and from the river unto the ends of the earth" (Psalm 72:8). Cf. Psalm 87. And Isaiah, with prophetic insight and vision, had spoken the words of beauty, comfort, and majesty, "And nations shall come to thy light, and kings to the brightness of thy rising" (60:3). Cf. Isaiah 54:1-3; Amos 9:11, 12; Micah 4:1, 2; Malachi 1:11. But never until the days of the New Testament had it become so fully clear that the Gentiles would enter the kingdom in goodly numbers (Matthew 8:11; 13:31, 32; Luke 2:32), and *on an equal footing* with those gathered from the ancient covenant people, the dividing wall having been broken down. Besides, not until the days of the apostles did these prophecies begin to be realized (Acts 15:14; Ephesians, 1:9-14; 2:11-20).

The main fact that should be emphasized, however, is that in the last century and a half (particularly since 1792) the missionary movement has been making great progress. The message of salvation in Christ which not so very long ago had reached only certain regions has by now rounded or nearly rounded the globe. Jesus says that it shall be preached in the whole world for a testimony to all the nations. *And then shall the end come.* This is a sign which is rapidly attaining fulfilment. We should take notice of this, and by means of work and prayer strive to bring the promise to *complete* fulfilment.

FOR DISCUSSION

A. *Based on This Chapter*

1. Describe the setting or background of Christ's predictions which are found in this chapter.

2. What two preliminary signs will precede The Second Coming?

3. Does the first of these signs indicate that everybody will have a chance to be saved?

4. What does it mean?

5. Will there be two Gospel Ages, one now and another after Christ's Return?

B. *Further Discussion*

1. Give a brief survey of the History of Missions.

2. Show that today this first preliminary sign is being fulfilled before

our very eyes, just as it has been in process of fulfilment ever since Pentecost. But *today* more than ever.

3. Describe the progress in Bible-translation and Bible-distribution in our own day and age. What can we do to promote this glorious work?

4. Why should we do all in our power to promote the great cause of Christian Missions, and this especially in our own day?

5. Does increased missionary enthusiasm necessarily mean that the denomination involved in it is sound and pure? Has increase in missionary enthusiasm ever accompanied decay in doctrinal purity? Give an example if you can do so. What is the lesson?

Chapter 25

The Second Preliminary Sign:
Satan's Little Season. What Is The
Great Apostasy?

Read Luke 17:26-37

1. Relation between "Days of Great Tribulation," "The Great Apostasy," And "The Reign of Antichrist."

The Gospel Age, during which the message of salvation is proclaimed in the whole world as a testimony to all the nations, will be followed by days of unprecedented distress. The reason why these days will be days of *great tribulation* for true believers, so that they will be grievously persecuted, is that ever so many people will *fall away* from the faith, which for a while they had been confessing with their lips. There will be a *great apostasy* or *falling away*. Read about it in II Thessalonians 2:3. Those who *have fallen away* will then begin to persecute those who *remain firm.*

At the head of this "falling away" movement will be a very wicked leader, the Antichrist. See chapters 27 and 28. Accordingly, "Great Tribulation," "Great Apostasy or Falling Away," and "Reign of Antichrist" are simply three terms that indicate the same final period of history which will immediately precede Christ's glorious return. It is also called *"Satan's litle season"* (Revelation 20:3, 7, 8).

The passage with reference to the coming apostasy by no means teaches that those who are God's genuine children will "fall away from grace." There is no such falling away (John 10:27, 28). It simply means that the faith of the fathers — a faith to which the children adhere for a while in a merely formal way — will finally be abandoned altogether by many of the children. In that sense the apostasy or falling away will be very real indeed. It will be on a large scale: *"many* shall stumble...*many* false prophets shall arise and shall lead *many* astray...The love of the *many* shall wax cold" (Matthew 24:10-13). History repeats itself; rather, prophecy attains multiple fulfilment, as was pointed out earlier. What happened during the reign of wicked Antiochus Epiphanes (who ruled from 175-164 B.C.) *toward the close of the old dispensation,* and again during the terrible siege of Jerusalem (A.D. 70), will happen once more on an even wider scale *toward the close of the new dispensation.*

2. Two Characteristics of The Great Apostasy

a. *False Security and gross materialism, followed by swift and sudden destruction.*

That is the gist of Luke 17:26-33. That section pictures the people of this final period. It tells us that they will be eating and drinking, marrying and being given in marriage, buying and selling, planting and building, just as in the days of Noah and just as in the days of Lot. As it was then, so it will be in the last days: the destruction will be so swift and sudden that the man who is on the housetop must not think that he will have any time to go back into the house to save his treasures. The man who is in the field better forget about returning home to rescue any of his possessions. Let the example of Lot's wife, who turned around, serve as a warning!

It is possible that you will ask in surprise, But what is there so wicked about eating and drinking, marrying and being given in marriage, buying and selling, planting and building? The answer is: though things of this character are not wrong in themselves, and though by means of them we can even glorify God (I Corinthians 10:31); yet, when the soul becomes entirely wrapped up in them so that they become ends in themselves and spiritual needs are neglected, they become a curse and are no longer a blessing.

b. *A Sharp Division between those who have fallen away, on the one hand, and the true believers, on the other.*

Of course, many of those who have finally abandoned altogether the faith of the fathers will still wish to pass as Christians (think of the present day radicals). But their very manner of living will show that they are not true believers at all. Moreover, the judgment which is going to overtake them very abruptly at Christ's return will show that they do not belong to the company of the elect. Verses 35-37 show this very clearly. These verses mean that when Jesus returns gloriously, two men may be doing the same thing: they are lying on one bed. Or, again, two women may be doing the same thing: grinding together. Yet in each case, *one* (the true believer) will be taken up, to meet the Lord in the air, while *the other* (the merely nominal believer, the one who has "fallen away") will be *left* to his terrible destiny: everlasting destruction. And this will not happen in *one* particular place, here or there. On the contrary, *wherever* apostates are found, destruction will overtake them. Viewed collectively, these apostates are here compared to a carcass, a decaying body (see Matthew 24:28). This is a metaphor, a figure of speech. Well, eagles and vultures are not very choosy with respect *to the place* where such a carcass is found. *Wherever* it is, they will devour it.

FOR DISCUSSION

A. *Based on This Chapter*

1. The final period of dreadful persecution is called Great Tribulation. By what other names is it called?

2. How can there be a Falling Away or Apostasy if it be true that there is no such thing as a falling away from grace?

3. What are the characteristics of the Great Apostasy, as pictured in Luke 17:26-37? Go into some detail on each.

4. Explain the passage, "Where the body is, thither will the eagles also be gathered together."

5. Who will be the leader of the Great Apostasy?

B. *Further Discussion*

1. What indications do you see in the church of today that could mean that the Great Apostasy is not far away? For example, do you find false security, materialism, rebellion against God's ordinances?

2. What can we do for our children, in order that they may not be swept away by this fast approaching evil?

3. Has there been any lowering of the bars in connection with such matters as the ordinance of marriage, worldly amusements, the confession of Scripture's infallibility over against such movements as

Barthianism? Is the church of today wide awake, so that it actually sees these evils, and does something about them?

4. Are church-members *today* as fully aware of the danger of apostasy as a former generation was?

5. Is grace inherited?

Chapter 26

The Second Preliminary Sign: Satan's Little Season. What Is The Great Tribulation?

Read Matthew 24:15-30

1. This Tribulation Must Not Be Restricted to Jerusalem's Fall

Great Apostasy and Great Tribulation coincide naturally. Now as to these days of "great tribulation," the reference is here not to tribulation in general (as, for example, in John 16:33 and Revelation 7:14), but to a definite tribulation-period. Jesus speaks about "the tribulation *of those days.*" He is very specific. He tells us, for example, that neither before it takes place nor afterward will there have been or will there be anything quite as terrible, and that for the elect's sake its days shall be shortened.

Just what does Jesus mean? Is He referring to a period of anguish and severe tribulation that will immediately precede the end of the world, or is he referring *exclusively* to the terrors that were to befall Jerusalem in and about the year A.D. 70, when Jerusalem and its beautiful temple were going to be destroyed?

Now, no one will find fault with the proposition that also in the present paragraph the distress that was to come upon Jerusalem was in the thoughts of our Lord. Note, for example, the statement, "Let them that are in Judea flee unto the mountains," and see also Luke 21:20-24. However, though during the last few years books have been written whose authors have tried to show that the distress of which Jesus here speaks refers to Jerusalem's Fall, *and to that alone,* having carefully read these books I venture to say, without the least hesitation, that this position is exegetically indefensible. It is open to the following objections:

a. If we thus restrict the meaning of the passage, then Jesus failed to answer the second part of the disciples' question, for in that case he would not have pointed out the sign *of his coming and of the end of the world.*

b. The tribulation-paragraph (verses 15-30) *follows* the prediction of the preaching of the gospel to the whole world (verse 14), which is a kind of dividing-line.

c. Verse 29 clearly shows that the tribulation of which Jesus is thinking *immediately precedes the second coming,* when all the tribes of the earth shall mourn upon seeing the Son of man coming on clouds of heaven.

d. The exalted language of verse 36 is also decisive against the interpretation which would *restrict* the meaning to the Fall of Jerusalem. Jesus certainly did not wish to convey the thought that not even the angels of heaven neither the Son knew when Jerusalem would fall.

e. Chapters 24 and 25 belong together. If the lofty language of Matthew 24:29-31 refers to nothing more momentous and final than Jerusalem's destruction in the year A.D. 70, then by the same process of reasoning the very similar words of Matthew 25:31-46 must be given this restricted interpretation. In both cases the Son of man appears in glory, and the people are gathered before him. But Matthew 25:46 proves that the end of the age has been reached, when the wicked shall go away into *everlasting* punishment, and the righteous into *everlasting* life.

But how can Jesus, in one breath as it were, refer both to Judea's distress and yet also to the final tribulation during the Reign of Antichrist at the close of the world's history? The answer is simple. In describing the brief period of great tribulation at the close of history, Jesus is painting in colors borrowed from the (prophetically foreseen) destruction of Jerusalem by the Romans. The city's approaching catastrophe is a type of the tribulation at the end of history. (What was said earlier on Prophetic Foreshortening and Multiple Fulfilment applies here.)

2. This Tribulation Precedes the Parousia (second coming)

There is still another difficulty. Even among those who *do* believe that this prediction refers to the end-time there are differences of interpretation. For example, many dispensationalists do not believe that The Great Tribulation will *precede* the Lord's second coming (parousia) but that it will *follow* this coming, and will take place when the church has already been caught up to be with Christ in the air. As they see it, these days of great tribulation on earth are for the Jews, not for the church. They are the days "of Jacob's trouble."

But this explanation is unnatural. Let any reader see this for himself by examining Scripture. Our Lord here in Matthew 24 is speaking about his *coming*—the very word *parousia* is used—at the end of the world (verse 3). In subsequent verses of this chapter he uses the identical word *parousia* (verses 37 and 39). Now when in verse 30 he speaks about "the Son of man *coming* on the clouds of heaven with power and great glory" is it not altogether logical to conclude that he is speaking about the same *coming* as elsewhere in this chapter? But now notice that in verse 29 we are distinctly told that this *coming* is preceded by "the tribulation of those days." *The coming follows immediately upon the tribulation.* The tribulation is accordingly a sign of the coming. Similarly Paul tells us (II Thessalonians 2:3) that The Great Apostasy (or falling away) and the revelation of Antichrist who afflicts God's children *precedes* the second coming. The two witnesses of Revelation 11 are persecuted, overcome, and killed during the "three days and a half" which precede their glorious rapture and the second coming. And also according to Revelation 20 Satan is loosed for a little season which *precedes* the return of the Lord upon the great white throne. Surely the most reasonable explanation in all these cases is to regard The Great Apostasy, The Reign of Antichrist, The Great Tribulation, Satan's Little Season (during which he is "loosed"), as referring to the same brief period, which *precedes* the one and only second coming of our Lord upon clouds of glory. Just as a tribulation (under Antiochus Epiphanes) *preceded* Christ's *first* coming, so another tribulation, even worse than the first, will *precede* Christ's *second* coming. It is clear, moreover, that the tribulation in question concerns not just the Jews but definitely *the elect* (Matthew 24:22, 24). Surely there are elect people who are not Jews! The tribulation will affect God's people "in the four corners of the earth" (implied in Revelation 20:8).

The question now arises: are there evidences even today that this Great Tribulation which will affect the entire church is approaching? Is it possible that some portions of the earth are even now entering this tribulation? What about believers living in those countries that are controlled by anti-christian governments? And what about all kinds of pressures even in so-called Christian countries, for example, to deny radio time to conservative groups? To make it difficult *for evangelicals* to build churches in certain districts? To try to force earnest believers to join organizations with whose practices they are in thorough disagreement?

Is it necessary to suppose that The Great Tribulation will come over the entire world *at the same time?* Is it not possible that between the close of The Gospel Age and the beginning of The Great Tribulation there will be some overlapping, so that the true state of affairs will *not* be this:

| *Gospel Age* | *Great Tribulation* | *Second Coming* |

but rather the following?

| *Gospel Age* | |
| *Great Tribulation* | *Second Coming* |

FOR DISCUSSION

A. *Based on This Chapter*

1. When Jesus spoke about the coming tribulation was he thinking *exclusively* of the Fall of Jerusalem? Prove your answer.

2. Will The Great Tribulation precede or will it follow Christ's second coming? Prove your answer.

3. Will The Great Tribulation affect the church in general or only the Jews?

4. Are there evidences today that this Great Tribulation is approaching?

5. Is it necessary that The Gospel Age has first completely ended all over the world before The Great Tribulation begins anywhere?

B. *Further Discussion*

1. How must the church prepare itself for The Great Tribulation?

2. Does Revelation 7:14 refer to The Great Tribulation of which Jesus speaks here in Matthew 24?

3. Does Scripture indicate anywhere how long this tribulation at the end of the age will last?

4. How will believers be comforted during that tribulation?

5. Why does the Lord permit his people to enter this tribulation?

Chapter 27

The Second Preliminary Sign: Satan's Little Season. The Antichrist. Who Will He Be? What Kind of Individual? How Will He Act?

Read II Thessalonians 2:1-5

1. Who Will He Be?

Let me begin by reminding you of the fact that what you are reading right now is not a *detailed* explanation. For *that* I would refer you to my *Commentary on I and II Thessalonians,* pp. 167-186.

Now here in II Thessalonians 2 the apostle warns the readers against being overly disturbed and acting as if the end of the world had arrived (see verses 1 and 2), and against believing that he himself had said or written anything that could have lent color to this notion (read what he says in verse 5). He declares that two events will occur first, namely, a. the apostasy, and b. the arrival of "the lawless one."

It would seem that the apostasy (discussed in chapter 25) will already have made some progress when "the lawless one" comes upon the scene. He "takes over" from there on, and makes a bad thing even worse. In him the movement of apostasy receives a very ambitious, energetic leader. He will be an active and aggressive transgressor. He is here called "the lawless one," not because he never heard of God's law, but because he openly defies it. The man who by the apostle John is called Antichrist (I John 2:18, 22; 4:3; II John 7) is by Paul called "the man of sin" or, more exactly translated, "the man of lawlessness."

Now when the question is asked, "Who will be he?" all kinds of answers are given. Some say, "Satan." Others, "the

129

beast out of the sea" of Revelation 13 and 17. Others do not want to think of *one* definite person at all but of many persons, called collectively "the man of sin." Some speak of "the line of Roman emperors," or of "Nero brought back to life." A very popular notion is that *the pope* is Antichrist.

From II Thessalonians 2 and from Daniel 7 it becomes clear, however, that the *final* antichrist, as pictured here by Paul, will be one definite person living in the end-time, a man in whom rebellion against God's law will as it were be embodied. He will be the great opponent, the terrible *adversary* of God, of God's law, of God's people, etc.

Now this man is called Antichrist, *not simply* because he will be a person who *opposes* the Christ, but because he will be a *rival Christ,* that is, a person who arrogates to himself the honor that is due to Christ alone.

2. The Description That Is Given of Him Here in II Thessalonians 2:1-4

a. *His perverse character (verse 3b)*

He will be the hell-bound, personal embodiment of the spirit of antagonism to God's law.

b. *His God-defying activity (verse 4)*

He will strive to dethrone God and to enthrone himself. In his reckless audacity and ferocious insolence he will exalt himself not only against the true God and against all so-called gods but also against all sacred objects. He will endeavor to wield dominion over God's people. Hence, for *them* it will be a period of great tribulation. He has his prototype in everyone who aspires to be God, for example, in the king of Babylon (Isaiah 14), in the king of Tyre (Ezekiel 28), and in Antiochus Epiphanes. In the days of the apostle John there were "many antichrists," that is, many individuals whose rebellious spirit foreshadowed the final and most terrible Antichrist.

FOR DISCUSSION

A. *Based on This Chapter*

1. What was the trouble with Thessalonian believers? That is, why were they so "shaken up"?

2. According to Paul, what two events will precede Christ's glorious return? Do these two events follow one another as two separate events, first the one, and then, when it stops, the other; or do they blend into each other so as to become one big event?

3. The man who by John is called Antichrist is called what by Paul?

4. Describe the character of Antichrist.

5. Describe his activity.

B. *Further Discussion*

1. The Thessalonian believers were "shaken from their normal state of mind" by the thought of Christ's return. Is that the proper attitude for a Christian when he reflects on Christ's glorious coming?

2. What had happened that caused these people to think that Jesus was coming back "any moment"?

3. Is the pope Antichrist? State your reasons for believing or not believing that he is Antichrist.

4. What is meant by "the little horn" of Daniel 7? And what is meant by "the little horn" of Daniel 8? Who was Antiochus Epiphanes and what did he do?

5. Are there "many antichrists" today? If so, what can we do to combat them? About what should we be more concerned: the coming Antichrist or today's antichrists?

Chapter 28

The Second Preliminary Sign:
Satan's Little Season. The Antichrist. How Will He Be Revealed? How Will He Fare in the End? What is His Relation to Satan and to Satan's Followers?

Read II Thessalonians 2:6-12

1. His Present Concealment and Future Revelation (verses 6–8a)

Paul tells us that, at the time when he was writing, the man of lawlessness was still being held back. Though present in the mind of Satan, *something* and *someone* for the time being prevented the Antichrist from appearing on the scene of history. We said *"something"* and *"someone."* It seems that Paul viewed the restrainer as being both a *thing* and a *person.* In verse 6 he says, *"that which* restrains," hence, some *thing;* but in verse 7 he says, *"one that* restrains," hence, a *person.* Perhaps he is thinking about *law and order,* as *the thing,* and about *whoever enforces* it (think of emperors and other rulers during the course of history) as the *person*(s). That at any rate is one of the oldest explanations. It also fits the context and is still being advocated by many of the best expositors. The spirit of lawlessness holds in its womb the lawless one. The devil can hardly wait until the day arrives when he can bring the final Antichrist upon the scene. When (at the beginning of the great apostasy) law and order, founded on justice, are finally removed, then the man of lawlessness will be made manifest. That is a logical explanation.

2. His Decisive Defeat (verse 8b)

The Lord Jesus, returning on the clouds, will intervene in the interest of his people. Messiah's very breath, the first gleam of his advent, will suffice to destroy the lawless one. The issue will be settled in a moment. There will not be a long drawn-out conflict, with victory now apparently with the lawless one, then with Christ, this "round" going to Antichrist, that one to Christ. The Lord Jesus will summarily and decisively put an end to Antichrist and also to his program.

3. His Relation to Satan and to Satan's Power to Deceive (verses 9, 10a)

The coming of the great opponent will be attended by astounding performances, aimed to delude the masses on their way to perdition. The energy of the devil will operate in and through the man of lawlessness.

4. His Sin-Hardened, Hell-Bound Followers and Their Destiny (verses 10b-12)

These followers are here described as "those who are perishing because they did not accept the love for the truth that they might be saved." The passage continues: "And for this reason God sends them a deluding energy, that they should believe the falsehood, in order that all may be condemned who did not believe the truth but delighted in unrighteousness" (my translation from the original).

When we read that God actually *sends* these people *a deluding energy*, we may feel that this is rather harsh. In explanation we would say the following. God is love. He is not a cruel monster who deliberately and with inner delight prepares people for everlasting damnation. On the contrary, he earnestly warns, proclaims the gospel, and even *urges* people to accept the love for the truth. But when people, of their own accord, and after repeated threats and warnings, reject him and spurn his message, then — and not until then — he hardens them in order that those who were *not willing* to repent may *not* be *able* to repent but may believe the falsehood that the man of lawlessness is God, the only God, and that everyone should obey him. In the final judgment all the deluded ones will be condemned. This sentence of condemnation will be just and fair; for those upon whom it is pronounced, far from consenting to the redemptive truth of God, have actually placed their delight in its very opposite, namely, unrighteousness.

FOR DISCUSSION

A. *Based on This Chapter*

1. What is probably meant by "that which restrains" and by "one that restrains"?

2. What will happen to Antichrist and to his program when Jesus returns?

3. Why will so many people be deluded by Antichrist?

4. Describe Antichrist's followers.

5. What will happen to them? Is this fair?

B. *Further Discussion*

1. How extensive will be the dominion of the Antichrist? Cf. Rev. 20:7, 8. What do you think of the idea that the restrainer is God? the Holy Spirit? Michael? the devil? common grace?

2. What is meant by the three days and a half during which "they that dwell on the earth" will in the end-time persecute God's children? Why "three days and a half," and not "seven days"? See Revelation 11.

3. Would it be easier today than it would have been a century ago for Antichrist to gain control over the whole world? If so, does this also show that we are approaching the day of Christ's coming?

4. What is the great comfort which believers experience when they think of the coming of Antichrist and of his terrible reign? See Luke 21:28; Isaiah 43:1-7.

5. Will the season of great tribulation for believers burst upon the earth suddenly or will it come gradually? Have some regions of the earth already entered it perhaps?

Chapter 29

Concurrent Signs. What Are They?

Read Matthew 24:1-13

1. The Difficulties

The historical background or setting of Matthew 24 has been summarized in chapter 24 of this book. Now when we examine the paragraph under study we notice that it refers to such things as wars, rumors of wars, earthquakes, famines (to which Luke 21:11 adds pestilences), and the rise of many false prophets. As has been pointed out previously however, the *primary* reference (here in verses 1-13) is to the events that were to precede the fall of Jerusalem. In our interpretation justice must be done to that fact. We have no right to begin at the tail-end and to lift the prophecy out of its proper setting. The question is legitimate, therefore, "If these wars, rumors of wars, earthquakes, etc., usher, in the approaching fall of Jerusalem, how can they in any sense whatever be signs of Christ's second coming?"

There is another difficulty which confronts those who would regard them as in any sense signs of the end of the world. It is this: *such things as here mentioned occur repeatedly in the course of history.* There have been ever so many wars and rumors of wars, earthquakes, famines, and things of that nature. One author has counted 300 wars, big and little, that occurred in Europe during the last 300 years. Was each of them a sign of Christ's imminent return? There have been violent earthquakes throughout the centuries. A certain writer counts 7000 during the nineteenth century alone. In the seventeenth century Robert Hooke wrote his *Discourse on Earthquakes.* There were a great many of them then. But even much earlier than that ancient historians, some of them writing before Christ's birth, wrote about the appalling number of earthquakes in their days. How then, we may well ask, can the occurrence of a war or an earthquake ever be a *sure sign* of Christ's return?

2. How These Difficulties May Be Solved

These difficulties are not insurmountable. As to the first, it should be borne in mind (see chapter 26 of this book) that Jerusalem's fall is here regarded as a type of the approaching end of the world. Read Matthew 24:9, 21, 29, and notice how Jesus, having spoken about tribulation in connection with the fall of Jerusalem proceeds immediately to discuss the great tribulation at the close of history. He cannot think of the one without also thinking of the other. Hence, if wars and rumors of wars, earthquakes, famines, etc., preceded the fall of Jerusalem, is it not logical to assume that they will also precede the second coming?

The second difficulty also yields to a solution. To be sure, in and by itself a war cannot be a sign of the end, for one never knows which war would be that sign. But our Lord in Matthew 24:33 has given us the key to the solution. He said, "When you see *all these things,* know (or y o u know) that he is near, even at the gates." In other words toward the end of the present dispensation the wars, rumors of wars, earthquakes, famines, pestilences *will occur together.* Not only that but they will occur *in connection with The Great Tribulation.* For both of these reasons they can be called *Concurrent Signs.* And they will probably be *more intense and extensive* than similar occurrences that have preceded them during the course of history. Thus, for example, Luke (21:11) speaks not about earthquakes but about *great* earthquakes. Matthew (24:11) predicts the coming of *many* false prophets. If all this be borne in mind, it would appear that these signs and wonders, considered not independently but in connection with The Great Tribulation, when they occur will by God's children be recognized for what they really are.

3. This Solution Is Logical for Still Another Reason

Is it not altogether reasonable to believe that terrible wars will occur in connection with Antichrist's rise to power? Are not wars often followed by famines and pestilences? And is it not equally reasonable to believe that The Great Apostasy will stand in very close connection with the sinister agitation of many false prophets?

FOR DISCUSSION

A. *Based on This Chapter*

1. When Jesus spoke of wars, rumors of wars, famines, etc., what was he referring to in the first place?

2. What are the two difficulties in regarding such occurrences as signs of the second coming?

3. How do you solve the first difficulty?

4. How do you solve the second difficulty?

5. Is the prediction with reference to these signs and wonders consistent with the prediction regarding The Great Apostasy and The Reign of Antichrist?

B. *Further Discussion*

1. Did wars and rumors of wars, famines, earthquakes, etc., actually precede Jerusalem's fall? Did false prophets also appear then?

2. When had Jesus ever told his disciples that after his departure from their midst he would come again?

3. Why did Jesus speak about "the beginning of travail"?

4. Are there any evidences to show that such things as famines and earthquakes are more in evidence today than formerly?

5. Does Matthew 24:11-13 imply that true believers can fall from grace and be ultimately lost?

Chapter 30

What Is the One Great Final Sign?

Read Matthew 24:3, 29, 30; Luke 21:25-28

The disciples had asked for a sign. Jesus had warned them that such things as wars and rumors of wars, famines and earthquakes would merely mean that "the end is *not yet*." "All these things are but *the beginning* of travail," he had said. They are only the beginning, not the end. He had added, "But when ye see Jerusalem compassed with armies, then know that her desolation is at hand" (Luke 21:20). So much as to the end for *Jerusalem and its temple, which in turn typifies the end of the world.*

As far as the end *of the world* is concerned, the Lord had given *two preliminary signs,* both of which we have discussed. The first was "the proclamation of the gospel in the whole world as a testimony to all the nations." The second was "days of great tribulation" (and of concurrent signs) which would be immediately followed by Christ's glorious manifestation. This great tribulation, as has been shown, stands in very close connection with the great apostasy, and is brought to its climax by the reign of the final Antichrist.

The reader will have noticed, however, that so far we have spoken only about two *preliminary* signs. These two are not yet *the one great final* sign. The disciples had asked about *the sign,* singular. They did not say *signs,* plural. Now, in Matthew 24:29, 30, the Lord indicates what will be that *one* all-glorious sign, and in the same passage and in Luke 21:25-28 he also points out the convulsions in the realm of nature that will accompany it.

1. The Convulsions in Nature

The picture is very vivid. While the earth is drenched with the blood of the saints in the most terrible tribulation of all time, all at once the sun becomes darkened. The moon ceases to give its light. The stars deviate from their orbits and race to their doom; they "fall from heaven." The powers of the heaven are shaken. Terrifying sounds are heard. There is "the roaring of the sea and the billows," causing perplexity among men. People faint with fear and with foreboding of what is beginning to happen to the world.

In connection with this apocalyptic picture strict literalness must be avoided. Until this prophetic panorama becomes history we shall probably not know how much of this description must be taken literally and how much figuratively. Observe, however, that the convulsions here described *do not blot out the human race.* Today, by means of sensational books and articles, we are being told that this or that frightfully destructive bomb *will completely wipe out humanity.* There are also scientists who tell us that the sun will gradually lose its mass — hence its gravitational pull — and that as a result the earth will recede farther and farther away from the solar orb and from its heat. Cold winds accompanied by blinding snow will cause the human race to freeze to death. According to another theory, however, some day a celestial body — call it a "star" or a "star-fragment" — will come whizzing toward our planet. Before it even touches the earth, buildings and homes everywhere will be a sea of flames, and everybody will be roasted to death. But according to the passages which we are now studying (also according to I Thessalonians 4:17) there will still be people on earth when Jesus returns! The souls already in heaven will regain their bodies and will quickly join God's children who are still on earth.

2. The Sign Itself

Suddenly light streams down from heaven. *The sign* appears: "And then shall appear the sign of the Son of man in heaven." Just what is meant by this one great final sign by which believers will know that Jesus is about to take his children unto himself? Some have thought that a special mark or emblem will appear in the sky; for example, a huge cross. But there is nothing that in any way suggests this. Far more probable is the view that *the very appearance of the Son of man upon clouds of glory is itself the sign,* the one, great, final sign *from the point of view of the earth.* Christ's brilliant self-manifestation will be a *sign* that he is about to *descend* in order to meet his people while they *ascend* to meet him in the air. This explanation gains some support from the fact that while Matthew says, "And then shall appear *the sign of the Son of man* in heaven," Mark and Luke leave out the word *sign,* and simply say, "And then shall they see *the Son of man* coming in clouds with great power and glory" (or: "in a cloud with power and great glory"). Remember also that the Lord told his disciples that *not* wars and rumors of wars, famines and earthquakes would mark *the immediate end* for Jerusalem, but that *the actual visible appearance* of hostile armies laying siege to Jerusalem would indicate that its desolation would be at hand (Luke 21:20). In both cases, therefore, we are dealing with *a sudden visible spectacle.*

But when Jesus appears in majesty, surrounded by a multitude of angels, upon clouds of glory, this will be to his people a *sign* in still another respect. It will not only mean that now "The Wedding of the Lamb" will most certainly take place, but it will also mean that this *Jesus* is, indeed, the *Messiah* of prophecy; for, the glorious manner of his appearance will correspond exactly with that which was predicted concerning the Messiah (Daniel 7:13, 14; cf. Matthew 26:64). This glory which will mark his appearance will be a sign, a definite proof, of God's delight in his Son and of the justice of the cause of him who was once the Man of sorrows and acquainted with grief.

FOR DISCUSSION

A. *Based on This Chapter*

1. Describe the convulsions that will take place in the realm of nature when Jesus returns.

2. Must all this be taken literally?

3. Will humanity be wiped out by these convulsions?

4. What is meant by the expression, "And then shall appear the sign of the Son of man in heaven"?

5. Name an Old Testament prophet who predicted Christ's glorious second coming. In what chapter of his prophecy?

B. *Further Discussion*

1. Will it be light or dark when our Lord makes his appearance?

2. Why is Jesus here called "the Son of man"?

3. What is meant by the expression, "And all the tribes of the earth shall mourn"? Is this the mourning of consternation and despair or is it the mourning of genuine sorrow for sin?

4. How will it be possible for people on both sides of the globe to see the Son of man coming on the clouds of heaven?

5. What time of the day will it be when Jesus returns? See the answer in Mark 13:35-37. What practical lesson does that passage teach us?

Chapter 31

Is the Establishment of the State of Israel the Fulfilment of Prophecy?

Read Deuteronomy 30:1-10

1. The Question

Very significant is the fact that in its journey around the globe — a journey generally from the East to the West, just like the sun — the gospel has made great progress, and this especially during the last century. Just as meaningful, however, is the fact that in the world of today and even in so-called "Christendom" of today there are various conditions that will make it much easier than heretofore for Antichrist to achieve world-dominion. That the stage is being set for the great apostasy can hardly be doubted. Such things as these should be considered signs of the times.

Many sincere Christians are convinced, however, that there is still another sign, a very clear and unmistakable indication that right now Christ's return must be very, very near. That sign, as they see it, is the establishment, May 14, 1948, of the state of *Israel*. According to one author: "The re-establishment of that nation in its own land, *even in unbelief,* is significant, indeed." By calling it "significant," he means that it is a clear fulfilment of prophecies. One such prophecy would be Deuteronomy 30:1-10.

All kinds of kindred ideas are afloat; for example, that *according to prophecy* the Jews will go back (or: have gone back) to Palestine, that large numbers of them will be converted just before Jesus returns, and that when this happens we shall know thereby that the return of Christ is just around the corner.

Two ideas, accordingly, must be discussed. The one is *Israel's restoration as a nation,* specially favored by God;

142

the second is *Israel's conversion*. The present chapter deals with the first matter. The next chapter will deal with the second.

However, since at present the attention is focused so generally upon the established fact that a certain number of Jews have actually established the nation called *Israel,* the first question will be cast in this form, "Is the Establishment of the state of *Israel* the fulfilment of Prophecy?"

2. The Answer

a. No one denies that there are many restoration prophecies; that is, many predictions of the return of the Jews to their land and their re-establishment as a nation (for example, Deuteronomy 30:1-10; I Kings 8:46-52; Jeremiah 18:5-10; Jeremiah 29:12-14; Ezekiel 36:33; Hosea 11:10). The point is, however, that insofar as these prophecies pertain to the literal restoration of the Jews as a nation, *they were fulfilled* when (in stages) the Jews returned from their Babylonian-Assyrian captivity, and were re-established in their own land. All this took place long, long ago, before Jesus was born.

That point is so easy to grasp that it is strange that many fail to see it. Let me illustrate. Say that here is a criminal, a Mr. Smith, who has been sentenced to *a year* in prison. His friend, Mr. Brown, visits him in prison and comforts him with the thought that he will be released from his imprisonment. Now, does Mr. Brown actually mean this, "Smith, you will be released thirty years from today, after you will have served *another* term in jail"? Such *comfort* would be nonsense. Similarly, you may be sure that when the Old Testament prophets predicted the release of the Jews from their captivity, their return to their own land, and their re-establishment as a nation, they were talking about a close-at-hand deliverance from Babylonian-Assyrian captivity, and not a home-coming from dispersion more than two thousand years later! As indicated previously, Old Testament prophecies must be studied from the point of view of their Old Testament historical background.

b. God does not reward disobedience but obedience. Hence, the deliverance predicted in the prophets was *conditional* in character. What the prophets meant was, "Israel will be restored *if it repents.* In that case its sins will be blotted out, and it will be permitted to return to its country."

See this for yourself in the passages which were mentioned a while ago: Deuteronomy 30:1-10; I Kings 8:46-52; Jeremiah 18:5-10; 29:12-14; Ezekiel 36:33; and Hosea 11:10. The language is as follows.

"And it shall come to pass *when* thou shalt return unto Jehovah thy God, that *then* Jehovah thy God will turn thy captivity."

"Jehovah will again rejoice over thee for good, *if* thou return unto Jehovah thy God with all thy heart."

"*If* they shall bethink themselves in the land whither they are carried captive, and make supplication to thee saying, We have sinned, and have done perversely, we have dealt wickedly, *if* they return unto thee with all their heart and with all their soul in the land of their enemies who carried them away captive, *then* hear thou their prayer and their supplication, and forgive thy people, and show them compassion."

"*If* that nation turn from their evil, I will repent of the evil that I thought to do unto them."

"*When* ye shall search for me with all your heart, I will be found of you, saith Jehovah, and I will gather you from all the nations...and I will bring you again unto the place whence I caused you to be carried away captive."

"Thus saith Jehovah, *In the day that I cleanse you from all your iniquities,* I will cause the cities to be inhabited, and the waste places to be builded." ... "They shall walk after Jehovah and the children shall come trembling from the west."

That this spirit of repentance was actually present at the time of the return from the Babylonian-Assyrian captivity is clear from such passages as Daniel 9:1, 2, 5, 6; Ezra 3:5, 10, 11; 6:16-22; 7:10; 8:35; 10:11, 12; Nehemiah 1:4-11; Haggai 1:12, 13, etc.

But the Jews who, on May 14, 1948, *established the state of Israel had not repented!* By and large their religion is that of humanism. It is a dependence on self, a "religion of labor." Dr. G. Ch. Aalders says:

"Whatever has happened in Palestine of late and whatever

may still happen there *has nothing whatever to do with divine prophecy.*" He means, it is not Israel's *restoration.*

FOR DISCUSSION

A. *Based on This Chapter*

1. What significance do many people attach to the establishment, May 14, 1948, of the nation of *Israel?*

2. To which release from imprisonment did the prophets naturally refer?

3. Show from Scripture that the promised blessings to Israel were *conditional* in character; that is, that God rewards *obedience, not disobedience.*

4. Does the present state of *Israel* fulfil the condition?

5. Accordingly, can it be logically maintained that the present state of *Israel* is a fulfilment of prophecy and that its establishment is a sign of the end of the world?

B. *Further Discussion*

1. How many Jews are there in the world today? Where are most of them living?

2. What happened to thousands upon thousands of Arabs when the Jews established the nation called *Israel?* Do you think that was right?

3. There are those who maintain that such passages as Isaiah 11:11 ("the Lord will set his hand again *the second time* to recover the remnant of his people") show that there is a national restoration of the Jews that belongs to the New Testament era. In the light of the context show that this is not at all what the prophet meant. Verse 16 clearly indicates what he meant by the *two* restorations.

4. Did Jeremiah in chapter 29 predict a restoration that is still future? See Jeremiah 29:10 and Daniel 9:2.

5. Does Daniel 9:27 (note especially the last part of that verse) support the idea that the Jews will again become God's favored people? Who *are* today God's highly-favored race? See I Peter 2:9, 10.

Chapter 32

What Is the Meaning of the Passage, "And So All Israel Shall Be Saved"?

Read Romans 11:17, 22-27

1. The Wrong View of This Passage

The wrong view, as I see it, is the following: In bringing the gospel, God is dealing with two groups. The one is the Gentiles, the other is the Jews. Now, for a long time the Lord deals *especially,* though not exclusively, with the Gentiles. There will come a time, however, when God begins to deal once more with the Jews. The result will be that "the great mass" of Jews will be converted, "large numbers of them"; one might even say, "the Jews as a nation."

My objections to this explanation are as follows:

a. It is contrary to the context of Romans 11. That context nowhere speaks about *national* salvation or even about *mass-salvation.* On the contrary, it speaks about *mass-hardening* and *remnant-salvation.*

b. Our Lord nowhere predicted a *national conversion* of the Jews. Jesus loved the Jews. He himself was a son of Abraham, Isaac, Jacob, and Judah. If the Jews are going to be converted in large masses as a sign of the end, one would expect Jesus to have said so, especially when the disciples asked him to tell them about the sign of his coming and of the end of the world. But he said the very opposite. He indicated everywhere that the privileges which once belonged to the ancient covenant-people would be transferred to a new nation (namely, the church), gathered out of Jews and Gentiles. (Read Luke 19:43, 44; also Matthew 8:11, 12; 21:32.)

c. According to the uniform teaching of Paul, special promises or privileges for this or for that national or racial group — say, the Jews, or the Dutch, or the Americans — do not exist in this new dispensation. (Read for yourself Romans 10:12, 13; Galatians 3:28; Ephesians 2:14).

d. God does not reward disobedience!

e. The text — Romans 11:26a — does not say, "And THEN all Israel shall be saved," as if the Lord will first deal with the Gentiles and, when he is through with them, will start thinking about the Jews once more. It says, "And SO all Israel shall be saved." The meaning of the word SO must be derived from the context.

2. The Right View

What the right view is, the context — so is seems to me — makes very clear. Paul in this chapter discusses the question how the promises of God to Israel can be reconciled with the rejection of the greater part of Israel (see verse 1). The apostle answers in effect: "You must remember that even during the old dispensation these promises were intended to be realized only in the lives of true believers. And that is true even today, that is, during the new dispensation." He says, "God did not cast off his people *which he foreknew* (verse 2) ... the seven thousand during Elijah's time (verse 4), ... the remnant according to the election of grace" (verse 5). One might have expected God to punish the Jews by wiping them out completely, or by sending upon *all* of them a *hardening*. The sin of nailing the Messiah to the cross certainly deserved that much. But the great *mystery* (see verse 25) is this, that this hardening is never complete. In each generation God gathers out from among the Jews *a remnant* that will be saved, certain "branches" that are grafted back into their own olive tree. Note, however: never more than *certain branches,* never more than a *remnant! Now, all these remnants put together constitute ALL ISRAEL. Alongside of* the process whereby *the fulness* (that is, the full number of elect) *of the Gentiles* is brought in, occurs also the process whereby ALL ISRAEL (all the elect from among *the Jews)* is saved. SO — that is, *remnant-wise,* as far as God's saving activity is concerned; *faith-wise,* as far as man is concerned (see verse 23) — ALL ISRAEL will be saved. SO, and in no other way; hence, *not as a nation,* but as a collection of remnants throughout the ages; *not* by continuing in unbelief, but by accepting Christ through living faith. In order to impart that salvation to ALL ISRAEL, Jesus came into the world (see verses 26 and 27).

I shall close this discussion by quoting from the works of three authors for whose convictions I have the highest respect.

Dr. Bavinck, the author of that monumental work, *Gereformeerde Dogmatiek,* says, "Accordingly, the term ALL ISRAEL does not indicate the people of Israel which will be converted on a large scale in the end-time; neither does it refer to the church out of Jews and Gentiles; but it is the 'pleroma' (fulness) which, in the course of centuries, is gathered out of Israel. It is Paul's prediction that as a people Israel will continue to exist alongside of the Gentiles; that it will not be wiped out or disappear from the earth; and that it will remain to the end of the ages, will contribute its 'pleroma' to the kingdom of God just as will the Gentiles, and will retain its peculiar task and position with respect to that kingdom" (my translation).

Prof. L. Berkhof, in his masterly work, *Systematic Theology,* says:

"ALL ISRAEL is to be understood as a designation not of the whole nation, but of the whole number of the elect out of the ancient covenant people."

And Dr. S. Volbeda successfully defended the thesis: "By the term ALL ISRAEL in Romans 11:26a, we must understand the total number of the elect out of Israel."

We are in thorough agreement with Bavinck, Berkhof, and Volbeda.

FOR DISCUSSION

A. *Based on This Chapter*

1. What is the wrong interpretation of Romans 11:26a?
2. Show that this view is wrong.
3. What does the passage actually mean?
4. What does the word SO mean here?
5. Mention three great Reformed authorities who share this view.

B. *Further Discussion*

1. In which sense are the Jews of today an indication both of the goodness and of the severity of God (Romans 11:22)?

THE BIBLE ON THE LIFE HEREAFTER   149

2. In which sense is the truth here revealed an incentive to missionary work among the Jews?

3. Explain the figure of the olive-tree and its branches (Romans 11:16-24).

4. What is human "hardening"? What is divine "hardening"? Is there any relation between these two?

5. What practical lesson can we draw for our own hearts and lives from God's dealings with the Jews?

Chapter 33

The Millennium: What Is Meant by "The Binding of Satan"?

Read Revelation 20:1-3

1. The Order of Events As Pictured in Revelation 20

The discussion of *The Millennium* belongs definitely to this Section on *The Signs,* as will become clear. It should *precede* the discussion of *The Second Coming,* just as it does in the Bible itself (Revelation 20).

With your Bible in front of you, opened at Revelation 20, and with eyes to read, this is really simple. *First* you read about *the thousand years.* The expression occurs in verse 2, again in verse 3, again in verse 4, again in verse 5, again in verse 6, and in fact again in verse 7. Hence, the wrong approach is, "I do not believe in the thousand years or in The Millennium (which means the same thing)." The teaching is right here in the Bible, and we should accept it! (However, this does not mean that we should be ready to believe in *anybody's* millennium!)

But notice the order of events: *after* the thousand years comes Satan's little season, for we read, "And when the thousand years *are finished,* Satan shall be loosed out of his prison" (verse 7). This "being loosed" is only "for a little time" (verse 3). Hence, we talk about *Satan's little season.* Again, Satan's little season *is followed by* Christ's glorious Second Coming, when he will be seated upon "a great white throne," and the dead, the great and the small, will be raised. We read, "And I saw a great white throne, and him that sat upon it, from whose face the earth and the heaven fled away; and there was found no room for them. And I saw the dead, the great and the small, standing," etc. (verses 11 and 12). As everywhere else in the Bible, so also here in Revelation 20, Christ's glorious Return is followed by the Final Judgment: "And they were judged every man according to their works" (verse 13).

So, here is the order, plain and simple: [1]MILLENNIUM, [2]SATAN'S LITTLE SEASON, [3]SECOND COMING AND RESURRECTION OF ALL THE DEAD, [4]FINAL JUDGMENT. Let us not reverse that order. Those who teach that Christ's Second Coming *will be followed* by a millennial reign are our brothers in Christ, to be sure. They mean well, and in the great battle against liberalism they, in many respects, are standing with us. But when they call themselves *Pre-millennialists,* meaning by that expression that Jesus is going to come BEFORE (that's the meaning of *pre*) the millennium, they are simply turning the order of Scripture around. Let us take the Bible *just as it is.* We are not afraid of Revelation 20. We love it! But we take it exactly as it is!

2. The Symbol Described Here in Verses 1–3

Do not *at once* begin to spiritualize or to interpret. First, see the vision *literally,* exactly as John actually saw it. Well, John sees an angel coming down out of heaven. He has a key with which he is going to lock the abyss. The abyss is a deep hole; that is, a shaft with a lid on top of it. This lid can be unlocked, locked, and even sealed. Upon the angel's hand lies a chain, the two ends hanging down. Evidently, he is going to bind someone in order to lock him up in that abyss. What happens? John suddenly sees the dragon, strong, crafty, ugly. It is "the old serpent," cunning and deceptive. John notices that the mighty angel overcomes the dragon. He binds him securely and firmly. In fact, so inextricably does he bind the old serpent that the latter remains bound for a thousand years. Having bound him, the angel hurls this serpent into the hole, and locks the lid over it. In fact, he even seals the lid.

3. The Meaning of This Binding of the Dragon

The dragon is the devil. His being bound concerns *the nations,* and not merely one particular nation. Passages such as Matthew 12:29; Luke 10:17, 18 and John 12:20-32 clearly show what is meant. Matthew 12:29 shows us (see the context there) that it was Jesus who in connection with his first coming (his victory over Satan in the temptation, his death on the cross, his resurrection, coronation) bound *the strong man,* namely, Beelzebub, the devil. In which sense? Luke 10:17, 18 and John 12:20-32 clearly indicate that it was in this sense, namely, that Jesus restrained the power of Satan so that he could not prevent the spread of the gospel to the nations of the world. It was when *the seventy missionaries* returned that Jesus said, "I beheld *Satan falling* as lightning from heaven." It was when GREEKS wished to see Jesus that our Lord exclaimed, "Now shall...the prince of this world be *cast out.* And I, if I be lifted up from the earth, will draw *all men* to myself." Note: "all men," not only Jews, also Greeks.

During the old dispensation salvation was almost restricted to the Jews. *Now* all becomes different. The church becomes international. The blessed gospel of salvation goes forth far and wide, and God's elect *from all over the world* are gathered in. This *Gospel Age* is the first of the two *Preliminary Signs.* See chapter 24.

The Thousand Year Binding of Satan means, therefore, that during the present Millennium or Gospel Age, which begins with Christ's first coming and (as far as the earth is concerned) extends *nearly* to his second coming, the devil is bound in this *one* respect, that he is unable to prevent the extension of the church among the nations of the world by means of an active missionary program, and that he cannot cause the nations — the world in general — to destroy the church as a mighty missionary institution. I completely reject the idea that the whole world will at length be converted or that through better laws, share-the-wealth-programs, etc., heaven will finally descend on earth. None of that! Satan will always be doing a great deal of harm. Within the sphere in which he exerts his influence he rages most furiously, just as a dog, though securely bound, can do a great deal of damage within the circle of his imprisonment. Outside of that circle, however, the dog can do no damage. So also Revelation 20 teaches that, although the devil can do much damage, yet with respect to *one* thing he is securely bound, namely, in the sense that during this Gospel Age he cannot prevent the chosen ones *from all over the world* from rejecting his lie and accepting the blessed truth revealed by

God in his Word. —There will come a "short season" when this world-wide marvelous missionary program will be thwarted, namely, the season of Antichrist, which has already been discussed. And *that*, in turn, will be followed by Christ's second coming.

FOR DISCUSSION

A. *Based on This Chapter*

1. What is the meaning of the word Millennium?

2. What is the order of events, or program of history, as pictured in Revelation 20?

3. According to Revelation 20 which comes first, the Return of Christ or the thousand year binding of Satan?

4. *Describe* what John saw, drawing a vivid picture.

5. What is *the meaning* of this binding of the dragon for a thousand years?

B. *Further Discussion*

1. What kind of millennium do the Premillennialists expect? Show that their conception is not in harmony with Scripture. See W. Rutgers, *Premillennialism in America.*

2., What is the Scofield Bible? Is a Premillennialist necessarily a Dispensationalist?

3. What is meant by the terms "Post-millennialist" and "A-millennialist"? Are you entirely satisfied with the term "A-millenialist" as a description of your position? If not, why not? Would you call yourself a "Post-millennialist" then? If not, why not? Are there different kinds of Post-millennialists?

4. How would you answer this argument: "The present increase in crime, the social unrest, the race-riots, the tense political situation, the great indifference to religion and in many cases the antagonism toward the church, — all these facts surely indicate that we are not now living in the era in which the devil is in any way bound"?

5. Granted, however, that we are now living in the age during which in *one* respect Satan is bound, what practical use should we make of this great privilege?

Chapter 34

The Millennium: What is Meant by "The Reign of the Saints"?

Read Revelation 20:4-6

1. Relation between the Binding of Satan and the Reign of the Saints

We speak of the Millennium *on earth* as "the Binding of Satan," and of the Millennium *in heaven* as "the Reign of the Saints." Verses 1-3, which we studied in our last chapter, concern the Binding of Satan. Verses 4-6 concern the Reign of the Saints. By "saints" we now mean the redeemed in heaven.

Of course, these two aspects of the Millennium − binding of Satan and reign of the saints − are most intimately related. It is in connection with the personal reign of our divine and human Mediator that Satan is bound so that his influence on earth is definitely curbed in *one* respect (as we have seen). It is in connection with this same personal reign of Jesus in and from heaven that the souls of the departed believers are reigning above.

Now in connection with this thousand year reign of verses 4-6, I shall endeavor to answer four questions: *When* does it take place? *Where* does it take place? *What* is its character? And *who* participate in it?

2. When Does It Take Place?

It has been indicated that *on earth* the Millennium or "thousand years" spans the period from the first to the second coming of Christ. No, *not exactly*, but just about. *On earth* the Millennium will stop just short of the second coming, for room must be left for "Satan's little season" (the period of great tribulation for the church, the season of Antichrist), which will immediately precede Christ's glorious return. Naturally in heaven there can be no such "little season." Hence, the reign of the saints extends all the way from the first to the second coming of Christ. Of course, it does not extend beyond that second coming. Why not? Will not the saints reign with Christ in heaven *even after Christ's return for judgment?* Indeed, but if you will carefully read verses 4-6, you will notice that this reign of the saints is actually the reign *of their souls.* After Christ's second coming, not the souls only will reign but *soul and body!* Hence, the Millennium in heaven extends up to the second coming and the resurrection, not beyond that point.

3. Where Does It Take Place?

The answer is: *where the thrones are,* for we read, "And I saw thrones and they sat upon them." Now according to the entire book of Revelation the throne of Christ and of his people is ever *in heaven.* Also, *where the souls of the martyrs live in their disembodied* state, for we read, "And I saw *the souls* of them that had been beheaded for the testimony of Jesus." John sees *souls,* not bodies. Such disembodied souls are living *in heaven,* not on earth. And also, *where Jesus lives,* for we read, "And they lived and reigned *with Christ.*" Now according to the Apocalypse the Lamb is represented as living *in heaven.* Hence, the thousand year reign takes place in heaven.

4. What Is Its Character?

It is a living with Christ: "They did live and did reign." In heaven these souls are pictured as taking part in all the activities of the Master. They stand with him on the heavenly mount Zion. They (symbolically speaking) follow him on white horses. They judge with him, constantly praising him for his righteous judgments ("True and righteous are thy judgments"). They have a share in his royal glory. Hence, they sit with him on his throne. They receive his name on their foreheads. Not only he but also each of them receives a golden crown, which they cast in adoration before his throne.

5. Who Participate in It?

First of all, the souls of the martyrs: "those who had been beheaded for the testimony of Jesus." Second, also all other believers who fell asleep in Jesus: "such as worshipped not the beast," etc.

FOR DISCUSSION

A. *Based on This Chapter*

1. According to Revelation 20 what two parts are there in the Millennium, and how are these two related?

2. *When* does the reign of the saints take place?

3. *Where* does it take place?

4. *What* is its character?

5. *Who* participate in it?

B. *Further Discussion*

1. How would you answer this argument: these *souls* are *people* (consisting of soul and body) who during the millennium will be living *on earth,* for in the Bible the word "souls" sometimes means "people," for example, "All the souls of the house of Jacob that came into Egypt were three score and ten"?

2. What is the meaning of verse 5: "This is the first resurrection"?

3. What is meant by "the second death," and by the expression, "Over these the second death has no power"?

4. What is meant by the statement, "The rest of the dead lived not until the thousand years should be finished"?

5. Will the end of the reign of the saints (as *souls* in heaven) be *a sign* for them? Of what?

Chapter 35

What Is Meant by "The Blessed Hope"?

Read Titus 2

1. Summary of the Chapter

Sanctification in mutual relationships, with emphasis on the Christian family, is the theme of this chapter. Doctrine and life must agree. Hence Titus must urge aged men to be temperate, dignified, etc.; aged women to be reverent; young men to exercise self-control (Titus himself being their model); and slaves to be submissive in their deportment, pleasing in disposition, and of unquestionable dependability. Moreover, Paul wants the older women to instruct the younger ones to love their husbands and their children, to be self-controlled, chaste, domestic, kind, and submissive to their husbands. All these classes should be motivated by the desire that the Word of God be honored, the sound doctrine adorned, and the enemy of the truth put to shame.

Not a single class or group must fail to come under the sanctifying influence of the Holy Spirit. Has not the grace of God appeared, bringing salvation to them all? This grace is:

a. *the Great Penetrator,* which invaded the realm of darkness and brought light — namely, the light of knowledge, holiness, joy, and peace ("salvation");

b. *the Wise Pedagogue,* training us to crucify worldly passions and to live lives of Christian devotion;

c. *the Effective Preparer,* pointing to the realization of *our blessed hope* when our great God and Savior Christ Jesus returns in glory; and

d. *the Thorough-going Purifier,* in Christ redeeming us from all lawlessness, and transforming us into a people for God's own possession, filled with a zest for noble deeds.

Titus must constantly talk about this glorious life of sanctification on the part of everybody. It should be presented to God as a thank-offering for his wonderful grace. Let Titus then see to it (by himself living that life) that no one slights him or his words.

2. Meaning of the Passage Concerning "The Blessed Hope" (Titus 2:13)

The apostle tells us that, trained by God's grace, we in the here and now should live lives of self-mastery and fairness and devotion

"while we are waiting for *the blessed hope,* the appearing of the glory of our great God and Savior, Christ Jesus."

Thus I have translated the passage in my *Commentary on I and II Timothy and Titus,* which may be consulted for details of interpretation.

It is "the blessed hope" for which believers are waiting. This expression "the blessed hope" means "the realization of that hope." By *hope* itself is meant earnest yearning, confident expectation, and patient waiting. This hope is called *blessed* because it imparts preparedness, bliss, happiness, delight, and glory.

Now, even *the exercise* of this hope is blessed, because of hope's immovable foundation (I Timothy 1:1, 2; Hebrews 6:19), glorious Author (Romans 15:13), wonderful object (everlasting life, salvation, glory, Titus 1:2; 3:7), precious effects (endurance, I Thess. 1:3, boldness of speech, II Corinthians 3:12, purification of life, I John 3:3), and everlasting character (I Corinthians 13:13).

Then surely *the realization* of this hope will be blessed, indeed! Now the realization of this hope is "the appearing in glory" (or "of the glory") *of our great God and Savior Christ Jesus.* As to this last phrase, the rendering in our Bibles (Authorized Version, text of American Standard Version) namely, "of the great God and our Savior Jesus Christ," is rather confusing. It does not clearly bring out the fact that Paul is here calling Jesus "*God.*" It must be stressed that the apostle is not talking about *two* persons but about *one.* He is saying that Christ Jesus is "our great God and Savior." It is thus correctly rendered in *the margin or footnote* of the American Standard Version and in the text of the Revised Standard Version.

The apostle's meaning, then, in the light of the entire context is this: our joyful expectation of the appearing in glory of our great God and Savior Christ Jesus *effectively prepares* us for the life with him. Now, how does it do this? First, because the Second Coming will be so altogether glorious that believers will not want to "miss out on" it, but will want "to be manifested with Christ in glory" (Colossians 3:4). Second, because this blissful expectation fills believers with gratitude, and gratitude produces preparedness by God's grace. If someone has conferred a great benefit upon you, you will wish to have everything ready so that you can give him a hearty welcome. When we think of the way in which Christ, having renewed our souls, is going to renew our bodies so that they will be like his glorious body, how he will receive us when we go forth to meet him in the air, how he will vindicate us in the final judgment, how we shall dwell with him forever in a gloriously renewed universe; and when, in addition to all this, we reflect on the fact that we had deserved none of this glory but only everlasting damnation, then, indeed, we by his grace will prepare ourselves thoroughly to meet him at his coming! Now read *Further Discussion*, No. 4.

FOR DISCUSSION

A. *Based on This Chapter*

1. How would you summarize this chapter (that is, Titus 2)?

2. In the present passage (Titus 2:13) does "hope" mean the exercise of hope or the realization of this hope?

3. Is Titus 2:13 a proof-text for the deity of Christ? Explain.

4. How does our joyful expectation of Christ prepare us for the life with him?

5. What is the meaning of "blessed" in the expression "the blessed hope"?

B. *Further Discussion*

1. Are you able to give a brief summary of the matters listed in the Table of Contents of this book, so that the program of the future, as revealed in Scripture, stands before you as a connected story? Try it.

2. When you await a visitor, you prepare everything for his coming: the guest-room, the program of activities, etc. Apply this to the manner in which we should await Christ's coming.

3. When Paul insists so strongly on calling Jesus "our great God and Savior," this was in reaction to what?

4. Does the believer's hope end in man or in God? In other words, is the realization of this hope limited to the joy which *we* shall possess by and by, or does it also include the element of *God's* glory and joy in our perfect salvation? Is the latter, perhaps, even the main idea?

5. What can be done to enliven and increase in our own hearts and the hearts of others that glorious *waiting for* "the blessed hope"?

Chapter 36

Who Will Come Again?
How Often Will He Come Again?
When Will He Come Again?

Read Acts 1:6-11; Matthew 24:36

In this chapter and in the next one we discuss the second coming. Now there are all kinds of border-themes; such as the Resurrection, Armageddon, the Rapture, the Final Judgment, the New Heaven and Earth. Such subjects we hope to take up later.

A convenient way to treat the matters before us is to ask the following six questions:

Who will come again?

How often will he come again?

When will he come again?

Whence and whither will he come again?

How will he come again?

Why (for what purpose) will he come again?

The first three of these questions will be taken up in the present chapter, the last three in the next one.

1. Who Will Come Again?

"Jesus, of course," you answer. And if I should say, "Yes, but in what capacity?" you are ready at once with an answer, "As Judge, of course." And that answer would be entirely correct. Correct, but hardly complete.

For the believer it is certainly comforting to think of him as coming again *as "Son of man"* (Matthew 24:30; 25:31) the One who *through suffering* attained unto glory, and who accordingly deeply sympathizes with his people who throughout the ages and especially during Satan's little season of great tribulation will have been *suffering* bitterly for Christ's sake. They will see him come in glory, as predicted by Daniel, and by himself when he stood before Caiaphas.

Moreover, he is coming again as *the Lord who comes to reward his servants*" (Matthew 25:21, 23).

He comes, moreover, as "*the Bridegroom,*" in order that he may take the bride unto himself.

Very beautiful is also what was stated in the section which you read from your Bible when you began this chapter. He will come as "*this same Jesus*" (or simply "*this Jesus*"). See the poem on this, in *Treasury of Poetry*, p. 404. Note also the passage: "And it came to pass, while he *blessed* them he parted from them" (Luke 24:51). So also, you may be sure that "while he *blesses* them," he will come again. Not only will it be "this same Jesus," but he will also come "in like manner."

2. How Often Will He Come Again?

Our brothers in Christ, the Dispensationalists, speak of *at least* two second comings: a first coming *for* the saints, a second coming *with* the saints. They also talk about *three* bodily resurrections; *three, four, five,* or *six* judgments; several places of torment; two chosen peoples; several varieties of evil beings; seven dispensations; and eight covenants (though not all dispensationalists agree as to the exact number of each). Now, if anyone thinks that I am just saying these things, get out your copy of *The Banner* (official weekly publication of the Christian Reformed Denomination with headquarters in Grand Rapids, Mich.) of May 18, 1934, p. 440, where you will find the evidence.

Now all this makes of the Bible a very difficult book. Here I would like to ask, "*How often* did Jesus ascend to heaven?" You answer, "Only *once*, of course." Well, then here is your answer (I quote from the portion referred to at the beginning of the chapter), "This Jesus, who was received up from you into heaven, shall so come in like manner, as y o u beheld him going into heaven." If he went into heaven *only once,* he will also come again *only once.* Nowhere does the Bible even hint that there will be more than one glorious return.

3. When Will He Come Again?

We know that he will not come until the proclamation of the gospel will have run its course (Matthew 24:14) and the man of sin will have been revealed (II Thessalonians 2:3), as has been explained previously. We also know that he cannot come again until the fulness of both Gentiles and Jews will have been gathered in; that is, he will come "when the number of the elect is complete" (II Peter 3:9; cf. Article XXXVII of *The Belgic Confession*). For the rest, all we know is that "of that day and hour knows no one, not even the angels of heaven, neither the Son, but the Father only."

FOR DISCUSSION

A. *Based on This Chapter*

1. What are the six questions discussed in this chapter and in the next one?

2. *Who* will come again; that is, what comforting names are applied to him in Scripture?

3. *How often* will Jesus come again?

4. In which sense is it true that Dispensationalists have made of the Bible a book difficult to understand?

5. When will Jesus come again? Will people be converted after his return?

B. *Further Discussion*

1. We have discussed the titles *of comfort* given to the returning Lord. But are there also titles *of terror*, showing in what capacity he will deal with the wicked?

2. Some treat Dispensationalism as a matter of complete indifference. They say, "Well, the last word has not yet been written or spoken about this." Do you think that this is the proper attitude for us to take?

3. According to Acts 1:6-8, what erroneous ideas did the disciples have concerning the establishment of the kingdom, and what did Jesus mean by the answer he gives them in verses 7 and 8?

4. Is it not true that Jesus knows all things? How, then, can Matthew 24:36 say that the Son does not know "that day and that hour"?

5. How did the Seventh Day Adventists arrive at their date 1844 on the basis of Daniel 8:14? What is the correct interpretation of that prophecy?

Chapter 37

Whence and Whither Will He Come Again?
How Will He Come Again?
For What Purpose Will He Come Again?

Read II Thessalonians 1

1. Whence and Whither Will He Come Again?

In order to give a correct answer to the question, "Where is Christ coming from?" it is well, first of all, to know where he went at his ascension. As to the latter, the language is clear enough. More than nineteen centuries ago our Lord ascended physically and visibly "from the mount called Olivet" (Acts 1:12). "As the disciples were looking, he was taken up, and a cloud received him out of their sight" (Acts 1:9). "He was carried up into heaven" (Luke 24:51). "He passed through the heavens" (Hebrews 4:14), and "sat down at God's right hand, far above all rule and authority and power and dominion and every name that is named" (Ephesians 1:21).

In such a description the exact line of demarcation between the physical and the spiritual, between the literal and the figurative, is hard to draw. One fact is clear, nevertheless, namely, that heaven is *a place* and *not only a condition*. And also another fact is not open to doubt: when Christ's human nature arrived in heaven, his body did not become diffused or distended all over heaven, neither did it become omnipresent. Similarly, therefore, when our Lord returns, he will return from the place which he last occupied in heaven. He will descend to, and will be seen coming upon, the clouds, and will then go forth to meet his people, while they too will ascend from the earth "to meet him *in the air*."

From passages such as Job 19:25, Acts 1:11, and Zechariah 14:4, some (for example Dr. Abraham Kuyper Sr.) have concluded that with a view to the final judgment Jesus will then descend *to the earth,* where, as they see it, "the great assize" will be held. Others (for example Dr. Herman Bavinck) express themselves less definitely, and simply state that the final judgment will require *a place where,* and *a certain amount of time during which,* it can be held. See chapter 43, point 5.

2. "How" Will He Come Again?

His coming will be very *sudden.* It will take people *by surprise.* A moment ago, "the sign" was not yet there. All of a sudden, there it is! (I Thessalonians 5:1, 2, 3).

It will introduce a series of events which will follow one another *in rapid succession.* Notice the language in such passages as I Corinthians 15:52 and Revelation 20:11.

It will be a *most glorious* coming: "the revelation of the Lord Jesus from heaven with the angels of his power in flaming fire" (verse 7 of the section which you read a while ago from your Bible). Jesus, together with a multitude of angels and of the souls of the redeemed, (I Thessalonians 3:13) leaves heaven.

It will be a *physical* coming, as has already been indicated.

Will this second coming also be *visible?* (Theoretically it could be *physical,* bodily, but still *not seen* by the eyes of men.) And will it be *audible;* that is, will there be sounds in connection with it, so that people will not only *see* it but also *hear* it? These two questions will be answered in chapter 42.

3. "Why" (that is, for what purpose) Will He Come Again?

Here are some of the answers given in Scripture: he will return in order

a. "to inflict vengeance on those who do not know God, even on those who do not obey the gospel" (see verse 8).

b. "to be glorified in his saints and to be marveled at in all who believe" (see verse 10).

c. "to judge the living and the dead" (Matthew 25:31-46; John 5:22, 27, 28; II Corinthians 5:10; II Timothy 4:1; I Peter 4:5; Revelation 20:11-15).

d. "to make all things new" (Revelation 21:5).

FOR DISCUSSION

A. *Based on This Chapter*

1. At his second coming, where will Jesus be coming from and where will he be going to?

2. Is heaven a place? Is Jesus *physically* present in heaven right now?

3. Who will accompany the Lord at his coming?

4. Describe that coming.

5. For what purpose will Jesus come again?

B. *Further Discussion*

1. Is there any difference between the Reformed and the Lutheran view of Christ's ascension? If so, would this have any bearing on the explanation of the second coming?

2. How does the parable of the five wise and the five foolish virgins teach that after Christ's return there will no longer be any opportunity to repent and be saved?

3. A cloud figured in Christ's ascension, and clouds again are mentioned in connection with the Lord's return. Do these clouds, in addition to their literal meaning, have any symbolical significance in Scripture?

4. What can we do in order to fill the minds and hearts of our children with true joy and gratitude whenever they think of Christ's return?

5. How will Jesus be "glorified in his saints" at his return?

Chapter 38

The Resurrection. How Many Resurrections?
How Will a Resurrection Be Possible?

Read John 5:19-30

When Jesus returns, he will raise the dead (I Corinthians 15:52). We now turn to a paragraph in which this resurrection is discussed, namely, the paragraph referred to above this chapter.

1. Meaning, in Brief, of This Paragraph

It was on the Sabbath that Jesus had healed the invalid at the pool of Bethzatha (Bethesda). The Jews had accused the healed man (and, by implication, also the Lord) of sabbath-desecration. Jesus had answered their criticism by saying, "My Father is working until now, and I too am working." The Jews had charged that, by saying this, Jesus was making himself equal with God. They had plotted to kill him. But the Lord now defends himself by means of an argument which may be summarized as follows:

a. In attacking me, the Son, you are attacking the Father himself, for what the Son is doing the Father is also doing.

b. Are you amazed because I healed this sick man? *Greater works* will follow, namely, imparting life to the dead and judging all men.

c. Do you question how it is possible for me to raise the dead and to execute judgment? I can do the former because the Father has given me to have life in myself, and the latter in my capacity as Son of man.

d. The proper reaction to my words and works is not base unbelief and hatred, nor even the attitude of mind that fails to rise above amazement, but *faith* which honors the Son even as it honors the Father.

167

e. Those who exercise this faith do not come into condemnation but have even now passed out of death into life.

f. In the final day, they — together with *all* the other dead — will also rise *physically*. But though all will be raised, there will be a great difference in *the character* of their resurrection. Those who have done good will come out of their tombs for *the resurrection of life;* the others, for *the resurrection of condemnation.*

2. With Respect to the Time When It Will Occur, There Will Be Only One Resurrection of the Body

For our present purpose our interest is centered in two verses, which can be rendered as follows:

"Stop being surprised about this, for the hour is coming when all who are in the tombs will hear his voice and will come out; those who have done good, for the resurrection of life, and those who have practised evil, for the resurrection of condemnation" (verses 28 and 29).

How many resurrections will there be? Some say, "Clearly two, for in this passage Jesus even names them. He calls the one *the resurrection of life,* and the other *the resurrection of condemnation.*"

Now we grant immediately that if the attention is riveted upon the great contrast between the body with which *the wicked* will arise and the body with which *believers* will arise, then there are, indeed, two bodily resurrections. But is that really all that is meant when dispensationalists talk about two or more resurrections? Indeed not. What they mean is that there will be *a time-interval* between the resurrections. It is in *that* sense that some speak of *two* resurrections (or resurrection-periods), some *three,* and some *four.* Blackstone, in his book *Jesus Is Coming,* pp. 72-74, accepts *a resurrection of the just* at the moment of Christ's "Parousia" *(first* second-coming), then *a resurrection of the tribulation-saints* at Christ's "Revelation," seven years later, and finally, one thousand years after that, *a resurrection of judgment.* This idea of *three* resurrections, separated from one another by intervals of time, is rather popular.

But this idea is clearly contrary to what we read in the verses which we are studying. We are distinctly told that *all*, both believers and unbelievers, will be raised *together*, that is, in that *one* hour. To be sure, no one knows just how long that hour will last. But one thing is important: absolutely no time-distinction is introduced either here or anywhere else in the Bible. When the hour strikes, *all* come forth. The *one* general resurrection comprises both the just and the unjust (see Acts 24:15). Martha of Bethany knew of only *one*, general bodily resurrection. She said, "I know that my brother will rise again in THE resurrection." She is, in fact, even more specific, for she calls it "the resurrection *at the last day*," and not "the resurrection that will occur one thousand years before the last day." And our Lord Jesus Christ, no fewer than four times in one discourse, tells us that he will raise believers "at the last day" (John 6:39, 40, 44, 54). *As to time*, therefore, there will be *one* general resurrection, not two, three, or four resurrections or resurrection-periods.

3. The Dead Are Going to Arise, But How Will This Be Possible?

Have you ever tried to imagine what this will mean: all those who ever lived on earth rising again? Also those martyrs who were devoured by lions, and those who were burned alive? The human mind can never fully penetrate this mystery, at least not on this side of the grave. A few elucidating remarks can be made, however. A *resurrection* is not the same thing as a *restoration* of all the elements that once belonged to our body. A *seed* or *kernel* of each body will be preserved, however. Now, out of and around this "seed" and in harmony with its pattern the Lord will build a body, exactly as I Corinthians 15:38 teaches, "To each seed God gives a body of its own." Thus every human body retains its own identity. If that were not true, it would be foolish to speak about "the resurrection" of the body. The Belgic Confession, article 37, is entirely correct when it states, "For all the dead shall be raised out of the earth, and their souls joined and united *with their proper bodies in which they formerly lived*." God Almighty can and will do this!

FOR DISCUSSION

A. *Based on This Chapter*

1. In what sense is it true that there are *two* bodily resurrections?

2. In which sense is it true that there is only one bodily resurrection?

3. Prove that, as concerns time, there will be only one bodily resurrection in which all, believers and unbelievers, will be raised.

4. Is *resurrection* the same as *restoration* of all the particles that once belonged to the body?

5. What does the Bible mean when it says, "To each seed God gives a body of its own"? What does article 37 of The Belgic Confession say about this?

B. *Further Discussion*

1. When Revelation 20:5, 6 mentions "the first resurrection," and accordingly implies a second resurrection, does this mean two *bodily* resurrections? What does it mean?

2. Does the expression "the resurrection of the body" imply that between our present body and that which we shall inhabit at Christ's return there will be identity of material substance?

3. Is the idea that a seed, kernel, or germ of each body will be preserved contrary to what science teaches with respect to matter and its disintegration?

4. How would you answer this argument: Scripture does not teach that of each human body a seed will be preserved, for the statement "To each seed God gives a body of its own" (I Cor. 15:38) pertains to the realm of vegetation (note the context), not to the realm of human bodies?

5. Is it more difficult to believe that *God will raise* our bodies than to believe that in the beginning *he created* the heavens and the earth and all that is in them?

Chapter 39

The Resurrection.
What Are the Two Striking Contrasts?

Read Daniel 12:1-3; I Corinthians 15:35-49

1. The First Contrast: The Resurrection unto Damnation Contrasted with The Resurrection unto Glory

Scripture says little about the resurrection body. This is true especially with respect to the bodies with which the souls of the lost will be reunited. Such passages as Daniel 12:2, Isaiah 66:24, Matthew 8:12, and Revelation 20:10b, are sometimes quoted as descriptions of the physical appearance of the reprobate after their bodies have been raised. But it cannot be proved that *all* of these passages refer *only to the body and its appearance.* Some of them would rather seem to tell us something about the agonies to which both soul and body will be subjected. Also, it is difficult to determine just how much in these lurid descriptions must be taken literally and how much figuratively. One fact can be affirmed without hesitation, however; namely, that these bodies will be a horrible sight, indeed. They will cause even the damned to shudder! Directly or by implication this horrible condition of the bodies in which the wicked will have to dwell forever can be inferred from the passages to which we have referred; especially when these are read as if they were *one* paragraph; as follows:

"Some shall awaken unto shame and everlasting contempt. Their worm shall not die, neither shall their fire be quenched; and they shall be an abhorring unto all flesh. The wicked shall be cast into outer darkness. There shall be the weeping and the gnashing of the teeth. They shall be tormented day and night forever and ever."

Now read what is said about the redeemed and *their* resurrection bodies:

171

"They shall shine as the brightness of the firmament and as the stars forever. We shall bear the image of the heavenly. We shall be conformed to the body of Christ's glory. We shall be like him" (Daniel 12:3; I Corinthians 15:49; Philippians 3:21; I John 3:2). What a tremendous contrast! On the one hand, sin and agony written all over the faces, and on the other nothing but holiness and glory!

2. The Second Contrast: Our Present Bodies Contrasted with Our Resurrection Bodies

This contrast concerns the bodies *of believers only*. The contrast is indicated in I Corinthians 15:42-44. Four points are stipulated:

a. *"It is sown in corruption; it is raised in incorruption."*

From conception to the moment when we breathe our last our bodies are subjected to the power of death. When we begin to live we also begin to die. And, in fact, even in the grave that process of corruption continues. But our resurrection bodies will be completely free from decay. They will be characterized by a freshness, vigor, and charm which will never depart nor even diminish! And since they will not be subject to death, it stands to reason that reproduction will not be necessary for the perpetuation of the race. Hence, the marriage-relation will cease. This does not mean, however, that the *spiritual* sex-characteristics which distinguish men from women will be eliminated. There is nothing in Scripture to show that the soul of *a woman* will cease to be exactly that. But as to *physical* relationships, we shall be like the angels, who neither marry nor are given in marriage.

b. *"It is sown in dishonor; it is raised in glory."*

If we had the opportunity to compare our present bodies with those of Adam and Eve before the entrance of sin, we would understand what Paul means when he says that our present bodies lack *glory*. And if that is true even now, while we are still alive, how much more true this will be when our bodies are "sown" in the dust of the earth!

By contrast our resurrection bodies will be glorious, for they will actually resemble Christ's own glorious body (Philippians 3:20, 21). We shall be *like him!* Consider for a moment that body of Christ: its effulgence, its beauty, its power. It was able to ascend straight into the sky, being carried up into heaven. And do we not sing:

"When *I rise* to worlds unknown,
  See thee on thy judgment-throne"?

c. *"It is sown in weakness; it is raised in power."*

The bodies in which we now live are weak from the cradle to the grave. But our resurrection bodies will be strong. We shall have eyes that never grow dim, ears that will never be in need of a hearing-aid, knees that will never grow feeble, hands that will never tremble. We shall run and not be weary; we shall walk and not faint.

d. *"It is sown a natural body; it is raised a spiritual body."*

At present our bodies are *soul*-controlled bodies; that is, they are dominated by our invisible essence, viewed as the seat of sensations, affections, desires, all of these polluted by sin. But in the future our bodies will be *spirit*-controlled bodies! That is, they will be willing instruments of our invisible essence viewed as the recipient of divine influences and as the organ of divine worship. By means of these bodies we shall glorify God forevermore.

FOR DISCUSSION

A. *Based on This Chapter*

1. What does Scripture tell us about the raised bodies of the lost?

2. How is this contrasted with what Scripture tells us about the bodies of the redeemed?

3. What is meant by, "It is sown in corruption; it is raised in incorruption," and by, "It is sown in dishonor; it is raised in glory"?

4. What is meant by, "It is sown in weakness; it is raised in power"?

5. And what is meant by, "It is sown a natural body; it is raised a spiritual body"?

B. *Further Discussion*

1. Should ministers ever preach about the condition of *the lost* at Christ's return? Should they *enlarge* on this — going into great detail — or should the emphasis be placed on the condition of *the blessed?*

2. According to Daniel 12:3, what kind of people will take part in the resurrection unto life? Is there a mission sermon in that text?

3. Why does Daniel 12:2 say, "And MANY of them that sleep in the dust of the earth shall awake"? Why not, "And ALL"?

4. Will the bodies of those who died in their infancy be raised in their immature condition, and will they remain in that condition everlastingly?

5. How does I Corinthians 15:58 fit in with the rest of the chapter?

Chapter 40

What Is Armageddon?

Read Judges 4:12-16; Revelation 16:12-16

1. The Question Which Har-Magedon Answers

In the preceding chapter we saw that the souls of those many unbelievers who perished in their sins will re-inhabit their bodies, becoming re-united with them in the resurrection unto damnation. In addition, there will still be wicked survivors (Luke 21:26), that is, reprobates who are still living on earth when Jesus returns. Under the leadership of Antichrist these have "just now" been subjecting the true Church to the most fearful persecution of all time. Just what will happen to these hosts of evil? It is to this question that Har-Magedon (or Armageddon) supplies the answer.

2. The Meaning of Har-Magedon in the Light of Its Old Testament Background

In order to arrive at the correct interpretation of the battle of Har-Magedon, we should first review the story in which this symbol is probably rooted. We find that story in Judges 4 and 5. Accordingly, let us retrace the course of history and mentally travel back to the period covered by the Book of Judges. This was a long time before Christ's coming into the flesh. What do we see? Israel is in misery again. This time King Jabin, the Canaanite, is the bitter oppressor. The spoilers go out to ravage the fields and to plunder the crops of the Israelites. So numerous are those spoilers that the Israelites have gone in hiding and are even afraid to appear on the highways (Judges 5:6). Wage war against the Canaanites? Ah, you do not understand. King Jabin and General Sisera are strong. They have nine hundred chariots of iron. And Israel? It has not even a spear or a shield (Judges 5:8). *Must* the people perish?

175

In the highlands of Ephraim dwells Deborah (Judges 4:5). Ask her whether Israel can defeat King Jabin and General Sisera. She will answer: *"No, Israel cannot, but Jehovah can and will!"* One day she tells Barak, the judge, "Up, for this is the day in which Jehovah is to deliver Sisera into your power. Is it not Jehovah who has gone forth in front of you?" A battle is fought. Where? At *Megiddo* (on a Bible map you can easily locate it near the brook Kishon, a considerable distance south-west of the Sea of Galilee). For the name of the place see Judges 5:19. In this battle Israel's foe is routed. And it was *Jehovah himself* who defeated Israel's foes: "Bless thou, my soul, the might of Jehovah...From heaven fought the stars, from their courses they fought against Sisera. The river Kishon swept them away, that ancient river, the river Kishon. O my soul, march on with strength."

Hence, Har-Magedon is the symbol of every battle in which, when the need is greatest and believers are oppressed, the Lord suddenly reveals his power on behalf of his distressed people and defeats the enemy. But the real and final Har-Magedon coincides with the close of Satan's little season. When under the leadership of Antichrist the world is gathered against the church for *the* final battle, and the need is greatest; when God's children, oppressed on every side, cry for help; then suddenly, dramatically, Christ will come, to deliver his people. That battle of deliverance after tribulation is Har-Magedon. It is for this very reason that in the paragraph which you read from the book of Revelation, and which describes this battle, you read, "Behold, I come as a thief." Also, in confirmation of our interpretation you will notice that Har-Magedon is the *sixth* bowl. The *seventh* is the final judgment.

3. What Happens to the Hosts of Evil in the Day of Har-Magedon?

a. Antichrist is discomfited (II Thessalonians 2:8) and, having been condemned, goes into perdition (cf. Revelation 17:11).

b. By means of the angels, the hosts of wickedness will be gathered unto the throne of judgment, where the wrath of God will be poured out upon them (Matthew 13:41; 25:41-46;

cf. Revelation 14:17-20). They will suffer everlasting punishment with respect to both body and soul.

c. The devil, that great deceiver, will be "cast into the lake of fire and brimstone." That "lake of fire and brimstone" is hell viewed as a place of suffering for both body and soul after the judgment day (though Satan himself has no body).

FOR DISCUSSION

A. *Based on This Chapter*

1. To what question does the battle of Har-Magedon supply the answer?

2. What story from the Old Testament furnishes the key to the understanding of the symbol Har-Magedon?

3. What, then, is meant by the battle of Har-Magedon, as this symbol is used in Revelation 16:12-16?

4. What happens to Antichrist, to his hosts, and to Satan as a result of this battle?

5. What is meant by "the lake of the fire and brimstone"?

B. *Further Discussion*

1. Who said, "We stand at Armageddon, and we battle for the Lord"? Did he use the term Armageddon properly?

2. Can you mention a battle hymn which seems to be based upon the Biblical symbol of Har-Magedon?

3. How do some dispensationalists explain Har-Magedon?

4. Just what is the relation between Har-Magedon and Gog and Magog (Rev. 20:8)?

5. What comfort do you derive from Har-Magedon, and of what duty does this symbol remind us?

Chapter 41

The Rapture. What Do Dispensationalists Believe?

Read Genesis 5:21-24; John 14:1-3;
I Thessalonians 3:11-13

1. Introduction

When Jesus returns, not only unbelievers but also believers will still be living on earth (I Thessalonians 4:15, 17). What will happen to these believers and to those who will already have died?

Among those who love the Lord there is a sharp difference of opinion with respect to this subject. In attacking the views of dispensationalists we want it to be understood that we are attacking their *view,* not their persons. As to the people themselves, they are our brothers and sisters in the Lord. It is not with them but with some of their views that we have a quarrel. Moreover, as far as the present chapter is concerned, we shall simply present their views, and do all our attacking by means of the second set of questions at the close of the chapter. What we shall have to say about the views of dispensationalists will be objective. Nevertheless, we hasten to add that among dispensationalists there is such a wide difference of opinion that any attempt to understand their views on the basis of our explanation of these views will be very unsuccessful unless it is constantly borne in mind that what is presented is the view of *many* — but by no means all — of these people.

2. Notes on the Three Passages Which You Have Just Read

Dispensationalists appeal to Genesis 5:21-24; John 14:1-3; and I Thessalonians 3:11-13, in defense of their theories concerning the Rapture. (Yes, they also appeal to I Thessalonians 4:13-18, but that passage will be discussed in chapter 42.)

Hence, a few words about each of these three passages will be in order. Genesis 5:21-24 comes as a surprise. Six times in succession we read, "And he died." Then suddenly there follows a brief biography of Enoch. For 365 years this man lived in close communion with his God. Nevertheless, he was no recluse or ascetic. "He walked with God...and begat sons and daughters." And then after these 365 years on earth, "God took him." Enoch never died at all. He was simply received up to heaven.

In John 14:1-3 our Lord is with his disciples in the Upper Room during the night of the Last Supper. Jesus comforts his disciples, telling them not to worry but to trust. He assures them, moreover, that though he is leaving them, he is not forgetting them, but that his very departure is in their interest: he will be preparing a place for them in the Father's house with its many mansions. He adds, "And when I go and prepare a place for you, I come again and will take you to be face to face with me, in order that where I am you may be also." This undoubtedly refers to Christ's second coming, at which time he will receive his own into his loving presence to abide with him forever.

I Thessalonians 3:11-13 contains Paul's prayer that he may be able to return to the Thessalonians. And he expresses the fervent wish that whether or not this desire be granted, the Lord may at any rate fill the Thessalonians with such an overflowing measure of love that their hearts may be strengthened so that there may be fruit for the day of judgment, when Jesus comes *with all his saints,* that is, *with all his redeemed.*

3. How the Dispensationalists Use These Passages in the Interest of Their View with Respect to the Rapture

Dispensationalists distinguish between at least two second comings. Hence, as they see it, there will be a *first* second coming, to which they give the name *the Rapture,* and a *second* second coming, to which they give the name *the Revelation.* In support of the *first* second coming they appeal to Genesis 5:21-24 and to John 14:1-3; and in support of the *second* second coming they appeal to I Thessalonians 3:11-13. Hence, they speak of a coming of Christ FOR his saints (the Rapture), and a coming WITH his saints (the Revelation). These are supposedly separated by an interval of seven years.

Dispensationalists tell us that the Rapture will be both invisible and inaudible (as far as men in general are concerned). One dispensationalist projects his thoughts into the future, and produces a newspaper — that is, an EXTRA — such as he thinks will come from the press the day after Christ's *first* second coming. This paper describes a man who, upon awaking, discovers to his horror that his wife is not beside him in bed! His daughter, too, has mysteriously disappeared. All over the city the story is the same: people of every social position have simply vanished without leaving a trace. These are the true believers who have been snatched up in order that for seven years they may enjoy supreme delight with their Lord in the sky. This is called *the Wedding of the Lamb.*

Now *on earth* during these same seven years the Lord begins to deal with the Jews again. They are brought back to their own country. Though at first many of them serve Antichrist, they (or many of them) subsequently see their error and accept Christ. But this means great tribulation for them. (Some of them will even be slain by Antichrist, so that when the seven years are over, there has to be a resurrection of tribulation-saints.)

When the seven years — that is the seventieth week of Daniel 9:27 — are over, Christ and his redeemed come swooping down from the sky for the great battle, namely, Armageddon (as *these* dispensationalists conceive of it). This is the coming WITH the saints (I Thessalonians 3:13). They swoop down upon Antichrist and his hosts, for the deliverance of those who during the seven years of tribulation have become converted. One author, himself not a dispensationalist but one who is thoroughly at home in their writings, says that according to the dispensationalists this battle will be one "in which are mingled saints, sinners, Jews, devils, discarnate demons, holy angels, glorified saints, Satan, and Christ, all fiercely striving amid blood, sweat, filth, dirt, dust, guns, swords, poison gas, tanks, and airplanes."

FOR DISCUSSION

A. *Based on This Chapter*

1. Do you regard this chapter an attack upon *people* or upon *error?*
2. Explain Genesis 5:21-24; also John 14:1-3.
3. What use do dispensationalists make of these passages?
4. Explain I Thessalonians 3:11-13. To what purpose do dispensationalists use this passage?
5. According to dispensationalists what follows hard upon the seven year Wedding of the Lamb?

B. *Further Discussion*

1. Does Scripture teach two second comings, separated by a time-interval of seven years?
2. Just where lies the difficulty in accepting the idea that people will be converted on earth during the seven year period?
3. Prove that Christ's one and only second coming will be both seen and heard.
4. What is wrong with the dispensationalistic explanation of Daniel's seventieth year-week?
5. Why is the dispensationalistic view with respect to the battle of Armageddon hard to accept?

Chapter 42

The Rapture. What Does Scripture Teach?

Read I Thessalonians 4:13-18

Having refuted the dispensationalistic conception concerning the Rapture, let us now see what Scripture actually teaches with respect to it:

1. A Rapture? Yes, but It Will Be Both *with* and *for* "the Saints"

The conversion of the Thessalonians was of very recent date. The danger of relapse into pagan beliefs and customs was not at all imaginary. One of these was the manner of grieving for the dead, as if there were no hope at all. But surely *for the Christian* there is hope. For him there is a glorious future as to both soul and body. Hence, the bereaved ones should "not grieve as do the rest, who have no hope." The apostle continues, "For if we believe that Jesus died and rose again, so also those who fell asleep through Jesus, God will bring with him." Notice: *with* him! The meaning is this: The same God who raised Jesus from the dead will also raise from the dead those who belong to Jesus. He will cause them to come along with Jesus from heaven, that is, *he will bring their souls from heaven, so that these may be reunited quickly, in a flash, with their respective bodies, in which they go forth to meet the Lord in the air.* When the Lord, as to his human nature, leaves heaven, these souls leave *with* him. But bear in mind: Jesus leaves heaven *in soul and body*. He "takes his time," so to speak. The souls, however, rush down to the earth to become reunited with their respective bodies. Then these resurrected persons quickly ascend, so as to meet Jesus while he is still "in the air." And so we see that our Lord comes *with* his saints, namely, with their souls and *for* his saints, namely, for their entire persons (soul and body). It is all *one* coming.

182

If the dispensationalists were right, the coming *with* the saints would be *seven years later* than the coming *for* his saints. Forget all about the seven years. Even then, these interpreters are putting the cart before the horse. It is *one* coming, but in connection with this one and only coming of Christ the *with* actually precedes the *for,* and not the other way around. For we read in verse 14: "God will bring *with* him" (those who fell asleep); and then, in verses 16 and 17 we are told that persons, their souls having been reunited with their bodies, are now *caught up* to meet the Lord in the air. Note: they *are caught up*; hence, it is by the power of God through Christ that they ascend, for Jesus has come *for* them, to be with them forever, and they with him.

2. A Rapture? Yes, but Definitely Not a Thousand Years before the Resurrection of the Wicked

Dispensationalists like to stress the statement, "And the dead in Christ will rise first." They interpret as if the entire passage were somewhat on this order: "And the dead IN CHRIST shall rise first; then, a thousand years later, the dead NOT IN CHRIST shall rise." However, nowhere in the entire paragraph does Paul say, "then the dead NOT IN CHRIST shall rise." Paul is thinking only of believers, of no one else. He is drawing a contrast between THE DEAD in CHRIST and THE STILL LIVING in Christ. On the one hand there will be those believers who at Christ's coming will already have died. On the other hand, there will be the survivors, children of God who will still be living on earth. What the apostle is saying, then, amounts to this: "Don't worry about your dear ones in the Lord, who have already died. In no sense at all will they suffer any disadvantage when Jesus returns. On the contrary, those who are still alive on earth will have to wait a moment until the souls of those who died have re-inhabited their bodies. In that moment of waiting the survivors will be changed in the twinkling of an eye. Then TOGETHER, as *one* large multitude, those who formerly constituted the two groups will go forth to meet the Lord."

So please place the emphasis on the right word, and read as follows: "And THE DEAD in Christ shall rise first; then WE

THAT ARE ALIVE, THAT ARE LEFT shall together with
them be caught up in clouds."

3. A Rapture? Yes, but Not Secret and Silent

Note the words: "For with *a shouted command,* with *a voice
of an archangel* and with *a trumpet of God* the Lord himself
(or "he, the Lord") will descend from heaven." This has been
called "the noisiest verse in the Bible." It surely indicates that
the coming of the Lord will be *public* and *audible.* For details
of explanation as to the nature of this shouted command, of
the archangel, and of the trumpet, kindly see my *Commentary
on Thessalonians.* Christ's return will be clearly *visible* (Rev 1:7).

4. A Rapture? Yes, but Not with a View to Any Seven-Year Wedding

We read, "And so we shall always be with the Lord." Please
note that word ALWAYS, not "seven years." Always with the
Lord! How wonderful that will be. "Therefore encourage one
another with these words."

FOR DISCUSSION

A. *Based on This Chapter*

1. Against what danger does the apostle warn here?
2. In which sense is it true that the one and only second coming of
Christ will be both *with* and *for* the saints? Explain.
3. Is Paul thinking about two groups, namely, believers and unbelievers, or is he thinking about two other groups; and if so, which two?
4. Prove that the Rapture will not be secret and silent.
5. Prove that the Rapture will not take place with a view to a
"seven year" Wedding.

B. *Further Discussion*

1. Explain the expression, "those who fall asleep."
2. Does Paul imply that he will be one of the survivors?
3. What are archangels? Name one. Are there others?
4. Explain the trumpet-blast: how and why.
5. What practical benefit do you derive from a study of Christ's
glorious second coming and our going forth to meet him? Should our
children be taught these things? Should you discuss them with dispensationalists, and if so, how?

Chapter 43

The Final Judgment.
How Many Final Judgments? Who Will Be
the Judge and Who Will Be Associated
with Him? Who Will Be Judged?
Where Will the Judgment Take Place?

Read Revelation 20:11-15

As has been indicated, the Millennium is followed, as far as the earth is concerned, by Satan's little season (see Revelation 20:7-10), which, in turn, is followed by Christ's return unto judgment, verses 11-15, about which you have just been reading.

The return itself has already been discussed. Hence, in this and the following chapters we take up the theme: *the final judgment.* We shall study this with respect to the following ten particulars: How many Final Judgments or Judgment Days are there going to be? Who will be the Judge? Who will be associated with him? Who will be judged? Where will the judgment take place? When will it occur? Why must it happen? According to what (or on what basis) will the sentence be pronounced and carried out? What will this judging comprise? And what will be the outcome?

1. How Many Final Judgments or Judgment Days Will There Be?

Our brothers in Christ, the Premillennialists, generally speak of three different judgments: a judgment at Christ's *first* second coming (Parousia), one at his *second* second coming, seven years later (the Revelation), and a judgment before the great white throne, a thousand years later. The first of these three, as they see it, concerns the living and the risen saints; the second concerns the nations (as to how they have been treating the Jews); and the third concerns the wicked. Some dispensationalists, however, arrive at four, five, six, or even seven judgments.

Scripture, however, always speaks of the final judgment as a single event. It speaks about *the day* of judgment, not *the days*. See, for example, John 5:28, 29; Acts 17:31; II Peter 3:7; and especially also II Thessalonians 1:7-10. From the passage which you have just read (Revelation 20:11-14) it is also clearly evident (see especially verse 12) that there will be *only one* final judgment.

2. Who Will Be the Judge?

According to our passage, the Judge will be "he that sits upon the great white throne." Again and again we read about "him that sits upon the throne...and the Lamb." Hence, God through the Lamb, Jesus Christ, will be the Judge. Of course, in all *outgoing* divine works (such as creation, providence, redemption, judgment) all three Persons of the Holy Trinity co-operate. Nevertheless, from passages such as Daniel 7:13, Matthew 25:31, 32; 26:64; 28:18; John 5:27; and Philippians 2:9, 10 it is clear that the honor of judging the living and the dead was conferred on Christ as Mediator, as a reward for his accomplished mediatorial work.

3. Who Will Be Associated with Him in This Final Judgment?

From such passages as Matthew 13:41, 42; 24:31; 25:31; II Thessalonians 1:7, 8; and Revelation 14:17-20 it is evident that the angels will be associated with Christ in the judgment. They will, for example, gather the wicked before the judgment-throne and will "cast them into the furnace of fire." They will certainly also take part in welcoming the Bride (the Church) as she goes forth to meet the Bridegroom (Christ).

It also appears from Psalm 149:5-9 and I Corinthians 6:2, 3 that believers will have an active share in the work of judging. At any rate, they will do so in the sense of praising Christ's righteous judgments (Revelation 15:3, 4).

4. Who Will Be Judged?

First of all, *all the fallen angels* will be judged (Matthew 8:29;

II Peter 2:4; Jude 6). This has reference to Satan and all his assistants, the demons.

Second, as is very clear from the passage which you have just read, all *human beings who have ever lived* will *together* appear before the Great White Throne. We read, "the dead, the great and the small." It is clear that none are excluded, neither the wicked nor the righteous. See also Matthew 25:32; Romans 14:10; II Corinthians 5:10.

5. Where Will the Judgment Take Place?

The answer is: "before the Great White Throne" (Revelation 20:11). But where will that throne be? Some place it on earth. According to others, however, there are two objections to this theory: a. in the book of Revelation the Throne (of God and of the Lamb) is generally in the upper regions, not on earth; and b. would there be room on earth, for all the generations that have ever lived, to stand *together* before the throne of judgment? But if not the earth, why not in the air? (This still would in no wise prevent Christ from "standing upon the earth" *after* the judgment). We know at any rate that at Christ's return believers will be caught up in clouds, to meet the Lord *in the air* (I Thessalonians 4:17). Why would it be impossible that believers go forth joyfully to meet their Lord and Savior, while at the same time the wicked are driven before the judgment-throne?

FOR DISCUSSION

A. *Based on This Chapter*

1. Will there be one final judgment or will there be several final judgments? Prove your answer.
2. Who will be the Judge?
3. Who will be associated with him in the judgment?
4. Who will be judged.
5. What theories are there with respect to the question as to where the judgment will take place? What do you think?

B. *Further Discussion*

1. What is meant by "books" and by "another book" in Rev. 20:12?
2. What is meant by "the second death" in Rev. 20:14?

3. Why has the work of judging been committed to the Son?

4. What do you think of the saying, "The history of the world is the judgment of the world"?

5. Does not John 5:24 teach that believers *do not come into judgment?* Please explain that passage.

Chapter 44

The Final Judgment. When Will It Occur? Why Must It Take Place? According to What Standard Will Men Be Judged?

Read Matthew 25:31-40; Luke 12:47, 48

1. When Will It Occur?

From the section which you have just read it is clear that the final judgment will take place immediately after Christ's second coming and the resurrection of the dead: "When the Son of man shall come in his glory...all the nations shall be gathered before him..." See also II Thessalonians 1:7-10 and Revelation 20:11-14.

Article 37 of The Belgic Confession says beautifully:

"Finally, we believe, according to the Word of God, when the time appointed by the Lord (which is unknown to all creatures) is come, and the number of the elect complete, that our Lord Jesus Christ will come from heaven, corporally and visibly, as he ascended, with great glory and majesty, to declare himself Judge of the living and the dead, burning this old world with fire and flame to cleanse it. Then all men will personally appear before this great Judge." See also Matthew 24:36 and II Peter 3:9.

2. Why Must It Take Place?

The objection is often heard, "The final judgment is entirely unnecessary and superfluous, for long before that time the reprobate will already know where they will spend eternity, and so will also the elect. Is it not true that when a person dies, his soul immediately enters heaven or hell? So, what possible purpose would a final judgment serve?"

However, this reasoning is faulty. Note the following facts

which show that the final judgment, at the last day, is indeed necessary: :

a. The *survivors* — that is, those individuals who will still be living on earth when Jesus returns — have not yet been assigned either to heaven or to hell. Hence *they* at least must still be judged.

b. But the final judgment is necessary not only for them but for everyone; for the exact degree, or measure, of weal or woe which anyone will receive *in soul and body* throughout eternity has not yet been designated. Up to the moment of the final judgment all those who have died have been in heaven or hell *with respect to their souls only*.

c. The righteousness of God must be publicly displayed, that he may be glorified.

d. The righteousness of Christ and the honor of his people must be publicly vindicated. When the world in general last saw Jesus, he was hanging on a cross, *as if* he were a criminal! This estimate — as if he were a malefactor condemned for his own personal crimes — must be reversed. All men must see him whom they have pierced. They must behold him in his glory...with his people "on his right hand."

3. According to What Standard Will Men Be Judged?

Entrance into or exclusion from the new heaven and earth will depend on whether one is clothed with the righteousness of Christ. Apart from Christ there is no salvation at any time (Acts 4:12; cf. John 3:16; 14:6; I Corinthians 3:11).

Nevertheless, there will be degrees of punishment and also degrees of glory. Note the expression "many stripes...few stripes," in the passage which you just read (Luke 12:47, 48), and see also Daniel 12:3; I Corinthians 3:12-14.

The degree of glory or of punishment will depend on two considerations:

a. What amount of "light" (knowledge) has this person received? (Romans 2:12).

b. How has he used the light which he has received? (Luke 12:47, 48). Has he been faithful? And if so, in what measure? Has he been faithless? And if so, to what extent? This will be evident from his *works*. Hence, we read that the dead will be judged "according to their works."

Now, this is true in a twofold sense, for these works will show both *whether or not* a person is a genuine believer in Christ, and also to *what extent* he has used or abused the light which he received (Revelation 20:13; then I Corinthians 3:12-14).

FOR DISCUSSION

A. *Based on This Chapter*

1. According to Scripture, when will the final judgment take place?

2. How does the Belgic Confession express itself with respect to this matter?

3. What objection has often been advanced against the idea of a final judgment?

4. How do you answer that objection?

5. According to what standard will men be judged?

B. *Further Discussion*

1. What makes Christ's words of praise for those on his right hand so wonderful? I refer to the words in Matthew 25:35, 36. Hint: read them in the light of John 15:5 (last clause); I Corinthians 4:7; and Ephesians 2:10.

2. How is *The Mystic Christ* revealed in Matthew 25:40?

3. What characteristic of a really good work is indicated in verses 37-39?

4. In the light of this section from Matthew 25 (particularly verses 35 and 36), would you say that we Protestants are at times in danger of underestimating the value of good deeds?

5. How can we teach our children to be a blessing?

Chapter 45

The Final Judgment. Of What Elements Will It Consist? What Will Be the Final Outcome?

Read Matthew 25:41-46

1. Of What Elements Will It Consist?

It is, of course, impossible for us to determine the *exact* sequence in which all the elements that comprise the final judgment will occur. Scripture does not give us sufficient information to arrive at such a detailed, precise schedule of events. There are, however, several elements which are mentioned in the Bible as pertaining to the final judgment. It is possible that, *in a general way,* the order in which I shall mention them will correspond to the actual sequence as it will unfold itself:

a. *Separation*

When all those who have ever lived will have been gathered before him, the Son of man will divide them into two groups, setting the sheep on his right hand, but the goats on the left (Matthew 25:31-33). Note that in Matthew 25:31-46 this is *the very first fact* that is mentioned. Here it should be borne in mind that God is omniscient. For God it is unnecessary to arrive, little by little, at any conclusion as to the inner condition of the heart that will characterize this or that individual. He has known it all along. Furthermore, are not the sheep those who are *elected* from eternity, and are not the goats the *reprobate* (also from eternity)? Besides, as was pointed out previously, by far the most of those who are gathered here before the throne of judgment have already been in heaven or in hell *as to their soul!* For these several reasons it will not be difficult for the Judge to divide the multitude *at once,* placing the sheep on the right, the goats on the left hand.

b. *Adjudication*

What has been said must not lead us to think, however, that the separation is *arbitrary*, so that, for example, it would be based solely upon the decree from eternity, and not take into account also man's actual life as it has been lived. On the contrary, the entire life of each person, including even his inmost thoughts and motivations, will be "brought into judgment." Thus the justice of the basic decision ("saved" or "damned") will become clear. Also, thus the degree of glory or of punishment for each person will be judicially determined. See Matthew 25:35-45; also Ecclesiastes 12:14; Luke 12:47, 48; Romans 2:16; and II Corinthians 5:10.

c. *Revelation*

Every deed which a man has ever performed, every word he has ever spoken, every thought he has ever conceived, every ambition he has ever cherished, and every motive that has ever prompted him to action or to inaction, will be laid bare, for himself and for all to see. In other words, "the books will be opened," that is, the complete record of each person's life, as this record exists in God's omniscience and as it is dimly reflected in each man's conscience, will now be made manifest (Daniel 7:10; Malachi 3:16; Luke 12:3; I Corinthians 4:5; and Revelation 20:12).

It is not necessary to assume that this will take a long, long time. By way of illustration let us think of a landscape in autumn. If you had to describe it in detail, it would take a long time to do so, but by means of a mere look or a comprehensive picture it can be flashed upon the mind in an instant.

d. *Promulgation*

The exact sentence affecting each person will be pronounced and the reason for it will be given. This is portrayed vividly in Matthew 25:34-46.

e. *Effectuation*

The sentence, whatever it may be in any given case, will be executed, carried out (Matthew 13:30).

f. *Vindication*

Throughout the entire process the justice of God will become fully evident. The righteousness of Christ, of his cause, and of his people, will be made manifest. Even the damned will be obliged to admit it in their inmost beings, and God's people will praise the Triune God for it (Revelation 15:3, 4; 19:2).

2. What Will Be the Outcome?

Read it in Matthew 25:46. However, as to the nature of the final state in heaven and in hell, see the next section.

FOR DISCUSSION

A. *Based on This Chapter*

1. If several persons are tried before an earthly judge, the division into two groups — guilty, not guilty — would take place *at the conclusion* of the trial. How is it, then, that when all men appear before the judgment-seat of Christ, the separation takes place *at once?*

2. Prove that men's thoughts, words, deeds, etc., will be brought into judgment. Why is this necessary?

3. What is meant by the expression, "The books will be opened"?

4. How will the sentence be pronounced and carried out?

5. How will the justice of God be vindicated?

B. *Further Discussion*

1. Will the *good* angels be judged?

2. Will the *sinful* deeds which God's people have committed be revealed in the final judgment? If your answer is "Yes," will that not make the final judgment a terrible ordeal even for believers?

3. If you cling to the opinion that the sins of God's people will *not* be revealed in the final judgment, then how do you explain such passages as the following: Ecclesiastes 12:14; Matthew 12:36; Romans 2:16; and I Corinthians 4:5?

4. Is there any significance in the fact that, while in Matthew 25 the *sinful* deeds of believers are not mentioned, their *good* deeds are recounted?

5. What light does Revelation 14:14-20 shed on the final judgment?

Chapter 46

The Final State of the Wicked. Does Gehenna Mean Annihilation or Does It Mean Everlasting Punishment As to Both Body and Soul When Jesus Comes to Judge?

Read II Chronicles 28:1-4; Matthew 10:28

1. The Origin of the Name "Gehenna"

As a result of the final judgment the wicked will be sent to *hell,* as to both soul and body. Now our English word "hell" indicates the place of everlasting punishment for the wicked. In the New Testament three words are used in the original: *Hades* (used ten times; see Chapter 17), *Gehenna* (used twelve times), and *Tartarus* (used once). Of course there are also such synonyms as "furnace of fire," "lake of fire," "second death," etc. But only Hades, Gehenna, and Tartarus are rendered "hell" in our English New Testament. Since we have already made a study of the word Hades, we shall now investigate the meaning of Gehenna, especially as it occurs no less than a dozen times. Also, Gehenna pertains to "the final state of the wicked."

Such a study is necessary, for we are being told that Gehenna should never have been translated *hell;* in fact, that there is no such place as hell. Gehenna simply means Annihilation, so say Jehovah's Witnesses (the Russellites). Now if that be true then all our English and American scholars who translated the Bible have erred grossly, for whether you read the Authorized Version, the American Standard, or the Revised Standard, you will find that in every case Gehenna has been rendered "hell" in the text of these translations. Has there been a concerted plot to deceive the Bible-reading public? Is everybody out of step except the Russellites?

Now the best way to study the meaning of the word Gehenna is to investigate its origin. Ge-henna comes from Ge-Hinnom, that is, the land of Hinnom, a valley belonging originally to Hinnom and later to his sons. You will find this valley on any good map of Jerusalem (just south of the city and curving toward the west). Originally, no doubt, this was a fine place, a beautiful valley. But it did not remain so. It was in this valley that a high place was built. It was subsequently called *Tophet,* meaning, according to some, "place of spitting out" or "abhorrence," according to others, "place of burning." Either interpretation would fit very well. It would seem that in the top of this high place there was a deep hole in which much wood was piled, and that this wood was ignited by a stream of brimstone (see Isaiah 30:33). The wicked kings Ahaz and Manasseh actually made their children pass through this terrible fire as offerings to the gruesome idol Moloch (II Chronicles 28:3; 33:6). Others copied their wicked example. (Jeremiah 32:35). Jeremiah predicted that the divine judgment would strike Tophet: God would visit the terrible wickedness that occurred in Ge-Hinnom with such mass-destruction that the place would become known as "the valley of slaughter" (Jeremiah 7:31-34; 19:2; 32:35). The God-fearing king Josiah defiled this idolatrous high place, and stopped its abominations (II Kings 23:10). Afterwards Jerusalem's rubbish was burnt here. Hence, whenever you approached the valley, you would always see those rubbish-burning flames.

Now by adding these various ideas represented by Ge-Hinnom — namely, ever-burning fire, wickedness, abomination, divine judgment, slaughter — it is easily seen that this Ge-Hinnom became a symbol for the everlasting abode of the wicked, namely, hell. Ge-Hinnom becomes (in Greek) *Gehenna,* the place of never-ending torment.

Lest the reader become confused, let it be stressed that there is only *one* place of everlasting punishment. Hades and Gehenna are one and the same, as far as *the place* is concerned. But when that place is called Hades, the reference is to the abode of *the souls* of the wicked *before* the judgment day; when it is called

Gehenna the reference is *generally* to the abode of the wicked, *body and soul, after* the judgment day.

2. Does Gehenna Mean Instantaneous Annihilation or Does It Mean Everlasting Torment?

The twelve occurrences of Gehenna are as follows:

Matthew 5:22: the man who says to his brother, "You fool," is in danger of "the Gehenna of fire."

Matthew 5:29; 18:9; and Mark 9:47: the man whose eye causes him to stumble must pluck it out and cast it away, lest his whole body, including the two eyes, be cast into Gehenna, the Gehenna of fire.

Matthew 5:30; Mark 9:43: a similar statement with reference to the man whose *hand* causes him to stumble.

Mark 9:45: a similar statement with reference to the man whose *foot* causes him to stumble.

Matthew 10:28; cf. Luke 12:5: God is able to destroy both soul and body in Gehenna.

Matthew 23:15: "twice as much a son of Gehenna."

Matthew 23:33: "How will you escape being sentenced to Gehenna?"

James 3:6: "The tongue...is set on fire by Gehenna."

Clearly, therefore, Gehenna is the place to which God sentences the wicked to be punished in both body (eyes, hands, feet, etc.) and soul.

Not only this, but Gehenna's punishment is *unending*. Its fire is unquenchable (Matthew 3:12; 18:8; Mark 9:43; Luke 3:17). The point is not merely that there is always a fire burning in Gehenna but *that God burns the wicked with unquenchable fire,* the fire that has been prepared for them as well as for the devil and his angels (Matthew 3:12; 25:41). Their worm never dies (Mark 9:48). Their shame is everlasting (Daniel 12:2). Their bonds, too, are everlasting (Jude 6, 7). They will be tormented with fire and brimstone...and the smoke of their torment ascends forever and ever, so that they have no rest day or night (Revelation 14:9-11). Yes, "day and night, forever and ever" (Revelation 20:10; cf. 19:3).

The passages in which this doctrine of everlasting punishment for both body and soul is taught are so numerous that one actually stands aghast that in spite of all this there are people today who affirm that they accept Scripture and who, nevertheless, reject the idea of never-ending torment. Instead of rejecting it, everyone should strive, by means of child-like faith in Jesus Christ, to escape it!

One hears the objection, "But does not Scripture teach *the destruction* of the wicked"? Yes, indeed, but this destruction is not an instantaneous annihilation, so that there would be nothing left of the wicked; so that, in other words, they would cease to exist. The *destruction* of which Scripture speaks is an *everlasting destruction:* (II Thessalonians 1:9). Their hopes, their joys, their opportunities, their riches, etc., have perished, and they themselves are tormented by this, and that forevermore. When Jeremiah speaks about shepherds who destroyed the sheep, did he mean that those sheep *ceased to exist?* When Hosea exclaims, "O Israel, you have destroyed yourself," was he trying to say that the people had been *annihilated?* Did Paul (Romans 14:15) mean to imply that by eating meat you can *annihilate* your brother? Or that he himself had at one time *annihilated* the faith? (Galatians 1:23).

What is perhaps the most telling argument against the notion that the wicked are simply annihilated but that the righteous continue to live forevermore is the fact that in Matthew 25:46 the same word describes the duration of both the punishment of the former and the blessedness of the latter: the wicked go away into *everlasting* punishment, but the righteous into *everlasting* life.

FOR DISCUSSION

A. *Based on This Chapter*

1. What three words that occur in the Greek New Testament are rendered "hell" in our English Bibles?

2. What do Jehovah's Witnesses teach with respect to the meaning of the word Gehenna?

3. Tell the history of the word Gehenna.

4. How do you distinguish between the words Hades and Gehenna? Do they indicate two different places, and if not what then?

5. Prove that Gehenna cannot mean annihilation, and that it does indicate hell as the place of everlasting punishment.

B. *Further Discussion*

1. What is meant by Tartarus and where does that name occur?

2. What is meant by the lake of fire and where does that name occur?

3. What is meant by the second death and where does that name occur?

4. In Revelation 14:9-12, what is meant by the man who worships the beast and his image, and receives a mark on his forehead or on his hand? Explain the rest of the passage (Revelation 14:9-12).

5. Explain Mark 9:43-48.

Chapter 47

The Final State of the Wicked.
Is God Present in Hell?
Is Hell's Fire Real?

Read Matthew 25:30, 41; Revelation 20:10, 15

1. Descriptions of Hell

There have always been people with a very vivid imagination. Some of them are adept at picturing the macaber. Whatever is gruesome to behold is their field of specialization, and they depict it in great detail. They will draw pictures of hell as if they had just come from there. Here, for example, in an old church hangs such a picture. It represents the morning of the resurrection. People are seen, coming out of graves. The devils are catching the wicked by their heels. Caldrons are hanging over hot fires. In each caldron there are fifty or more people. Demons are poking the fires. Pitiable characters, hanging on hooks by their tongues, are being lashed most unmercifully.

In his famous *Inferno*, Dante by means of the written word also drew pictures. However, Dante was a real artist, a genius. That man had originality. For example, with rare skill he adapted the specific punishment of hell to the nature of the sin. Thus, those people who had spent their lives on earth constantly quarreling with each other and avenging themselves were now in hell, forever tearing one another to pieces:

> "They smote each other not alone with hands,
> But with the head and with the breast and feet,
> Tearing each other piecemeal with their teeth."

Also, according to Dante, Satan, being himself the arch-traitor was forever consuming in his three mouths the lesser traitors Judas, Brutus, and Cassius.

The Middle Ages reveled in things of this kind. When we now turn to the Bible we find that it is far more sober and restrained in its representations. To be sure, it does indicate the nature of hell's punishment, but its main purpose even then is to warn the sinner to flee from the wrath of God by finding in Christ a sure place of refuge.

It has been shown in the preceding chapter that hell means *everlasting destruction*. The remaining items in Scripture's description of the abode of the wicked will now be summarized. In the summary which follows it must be constantly borne in mind, as shown earlier, that hell's most dreadful torment is for those who, though they knew the way, rejected it. Not as if for anyone hell would be a rather pleasant place. Far from it. It remains for all who enter there a place of despair and gloom, but certainly not in the same degree for all.

The remaining descriptive items can be briefly summarized by means of four words which may be arranged in two *parallel* or in two *chiastic* pairs, as follows:

(a) *away from*   (c) *fire*
(b) *together with*   (d) *darkness*

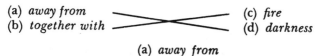

(a) *away from*

The wicked will suffer everlasting destruction "*away from* the face of the Lord and from the glory of his might" (II Thessalonians 1:9). They will "*go away* into everlasting punishment" (Matthew 25:46). They will hear the terrible words, "*Depart from* me" (Matthew 7:23; 25:41; Luke 13:27). Their dwelling-place will be "*outside*" the banquet-hall, the wedding-feast, the shut door (Matthew 8:11, 12; 22:13; 25:10-13). Within is the bridegroom. Within are also those who accepted the invitation. *Outside* are the sons of the kingdom who, having spurned the gracious summons, are knocking at the door in vain (Luke 13:28). *Outside* are dogs (Revelation 22:15). Wicked spirits are cast down ...down...down...into *the bottomless pit* (Revelation 9:1, 2, 11; cf. 11:7; 17:8; 20:1, 3). Thus they sink *away* endlessly *from* the presence of God and of the Lamb.

(b) *together with*

Yet, the punishment of hell is by no means only a matter of

202 THE BIBLE ON THE LIFE HEREAFTER

separation. It is also the very opposite, namely, a *togetherness,* the most gruesome togetherness imaginable. The wicked will dwell forever with the devil and his angels (Matthew 25:41; Revelation 20:10, 15). There is no love in hell (Isaiah 14:9-11).

(c) *fire*

That hell is a place of fire or of the flame is the language of Scripture throughout (Isaiah 33:14; 66:24; Matthew 3:12; 5:22; 13:40, 42, 50; 18:8, 9; 25:41; Mark 9:43-48; Luke 3:17; 16:19-31; Jude 7; Revelation 14:10; 19:20; 20:10, 14, 15; 21:8. This fire is unquenchable. It devours forever and ever.

(d) *darkness*

Lastly, hell is also the abode where darkness dwells. It is for some the place of *"outer* darkness" (Matthew 8:12; 22:13; 25:30). It is the place where evil spirits are kept "in everlasting chains under darkness" (Jude 6). "The gloom of darkness" has been "reserved forever" for wandering stars who cast up the foam of their own shame (Jude 13).

The four items can also be arranged chiastically: *away from* God, the Light, means *into the darkness.* And *together with* the devil and his angels means together with them *in the fire which has been prepared for them.*

2. This Description Gives Rise to Two Questions, Closely Related

a. *Is God present in hell? and*

b. *Is hell's fire real?*

As to the first question, this may be expanded as follows: How is it possible for the wicked to be sent *away from* the presence of the Lord? Is not God omnipresent? (Psalm 139:7-12). The answer is this: although God is indeed present everywhere, that presence is not everywhere a presence of love. Hell is hell because God is there, God *in all his wrath* (Hebrews 12:29; Revelation 6:16). Heaven is heaven because God is there, God *in all his love.* It is from this presence *of love* that the wicked are banished forever.

As to the second question, this can be rephrased as follows. If hell be the place of *fire,* how can it also be the place of *darkness?* Or vice versa. Are not these two mutually exclusive?

My answer would be, not necessarily. I happen to know someone who at one time by a certain form of radiation was seriously *burned*, though when this took place that person was in a *dark* room. And do we not also speak about *burning* thirst, *burning* fever, etc.? It is therefore entirely possible that in some *literal* or, if you prefer, *semi-literal* but nevertheless *physical* sense hell is the place *of the flame;* that is, *of burning*, even though it is also the abode of *darkness.*

Those who *deny* this point to the parable recorded in Luke 16:19-31. But granted that in his *disembodied* state the rich man was not being burned *physically*, does this in any way prove that when once the wicked receive their bodies they will not be tortured by a fire which in some sense is physical? It should be born in mind that the rich man in the parable is pictured *as if* he had a body (for example, he asks that his *tongue* may be cooled). In that *as-if-body* he suffers torment "in this flame." How this in any way proves that hell cannot be *the place* of the flame I fail to understand. The parable would rather seem to teach that terrible punishment, first as to the soul, but later also as to the body, awaits the wicked. And is not that the teaching of Scripture throughout?

But though the idea of a literal fire — that is, a fire which in some sense is physical — need not be excluded, it remains true that according to Scripture *the literal sense does not exhaust the concept. Everlasting fire* has been prepared "for the devil and his angels," yet these are *spirits*. Also, Scripture often associates two other concepts with that of fire, namely, *the divine wrath* and consequently *anguish* for the wicked. See this for yourself by examining such passages as Genesis 18:20, cf. 19:24; Deuteronomy 32:22; Psalm 11:6; 18:8; 21:9; 97:3; 140:10; Jeremiah 4:4; Amos 1:4, 7, 10, etc.; Nahum 1:6; Malachi 3:2; and Revelation 14:10, 11.

It was on Calvary, particularly as a result of the anguish endured during the three hours of *darkness*, that the *fire* of God's *wrath* for the sins of his people finally caused Jesus to cry out, "My God, my God why has thou forsaken me"? By descending into this *hell*, he delivered us from the greatest evil and placed in our possession the greatest blessing.

FOR DISCUSSION

A. *Based on This Chapter*

1. In addition to what has been said in the *preceding* chapter (Chapter 46) what are the four key-words which summarize Scripture's portrait of hell?

2. Away from what, from whom, into what? Together with whom?

3. Prove that Scripture teaches that hell is a place both of fire and of darkness.

4. Is God present in hell, and if so in what sense?

5. Is hell's fire real? Explain.

B. *Further Discussion*

1. Is hell's *darkness* to be taken literally?

2. Does the literal meaning, if correct, *exhaust* the concept *darkness,* when applied to hell?

3. What does it mean that Jesus "descended into hell"? Is that expression found in the Bible? Is *the idea* in harmony with Scripture?

4. How does Calvary shed light on the nature of hell?

5. "Only the damned in hell know how deeply Jesus suffered when he died for us on the cross." True or false?

Chapter 48

The Final State of the Righteous.
What Will the New Universe Be Like?

*Read Isaiah 11:6-9; Romans 8:18-22;
II Peter 3:13*

It would seem that when both heaven and earth will be momentarily depopulated — Christ and his angels, together with the souls of the redeemed descending from heaven; believers thereupon ascending from the earth to meet their Lord in the air; unbelievers being *driven* before Christ's throne of judgment (in the air?) — the universe will be subjected to a glorious process of transformation, so that out of the old "heaven and earth" a new "heaven and earth" will come forth. We read, "And I saw a great white throne, and him that sat upon it, from whose face the earth and heaven fled away; and there was found no place for them" (Revelation 20:11).

This process of transformation has four aspects:

1. The Great Conflagration

The heavens that now are and the earth have been stored up for fire, so that by and by the heavens being on fire — divinely ignited! — will be dissolved and the elements will melt with fervent heat. From the entire universe (with the sole exception of hell) every stain of sin and every trace of the curse will be removed (II Peter 3:7, 11, 12).

2. The Glorious Rejuvenation

The fire will not *do away with* the universe. After the fire there will still be the same "heaven and earth," but gloriously renewed, as explained in II Peter 3:13; Revelation 21:1-5:

"But according to his promise, we look for new heavens and a new earth, in which righteousness dwells."

"And I saw a new heaven and a new earth, for the first heaven and the first earth had passed away; and the sea was no more. And I saw the holy city, new Jerusalem, coming down out of heaven from God, made ready as a bride adorned for her husband. And I heard a great voice out of the throne saying, Behold, the tabernacle of God is with men, and he will dwell with them, and they shall be his people, and God himself will be with them, and be their God: and he will wipe away every tear from their eyes; and death shall be no more; neither shall there be mourning, nor crying, nor pain any more for the former things have passed away. And he who sat on the throne said, Behold, I make all things new. And he said, Write: for these things are reliable and true."

3. The Wonderful Self-realization

This organic realm will attain to complete self-expression or "liberty." It is that thought which is beautifully expressed in Romans 8:18-22. In that passage the apostle tells us that at present the creation is subjected to "vanity." Now this word "vanity" does not here mean "shallow pride" or "saucy airs." It has no reference to ambitious display, as when we say, "What a *vain* fellow this is!" It means *futility*, lack of effectiveness (cf. Ecclesiastes 12:8). It indicates that at present, as a result of man's sin, Nature does not attain to self-realization: its potentialities are cribbed, cabined, and confined. It is subject to arrested development. Though it aspires, it is not able to achieve. It may be compared to a very powerful man, a world-champion boxer or wrestler, who is chained in such a manner that he cannot make use of his tremendous physical prowess. Thus it is with the present universe, which lies under the curse. Plant disease decimates the crops, etc. What a glorious day it will be when all restraints which are due to sin will have been removed, and we shall see this wonderful creation finally coming into its own, attaining unto "the glorious liberty of the children of God," and no longer subject to *futility*.

4. The Perfect Harmonization

At present Nature can be described as "raw in tooth and claw." Peace and harmony are lacking in many respects. Various organisms seem to be working at cross purposes. It cannot be truly said that Nature is to any great extent man's willing servant. Fear and dread rest heavily upon the various conflicting domains of this universe. There is warfare everywhere. But *then* all Nature, gloriously transformed, will sing a symphony. There will be variation, to be sure, but a most delightful blending of sounds, colors, purposes, so that the total effect will be unity. And the prophecy of Isaiah 11:6-9 will reach its *ultimate* fulfilment. (We do not in any way deny that, according to the context of the Isaiah passage, there is an anticipatory fulfilment in the *present* dispensation, ushered in by the coming of Christ into the flesh.)

It is this final harmony which is set forth in *symbolic language* (please note the qualification) in the words, "And the wolf shall dwell with the lamb, and the leopard shall lie down with the kid...They shall not hurt nor destroy in all my holy mountain; for the earth shall be full of the knowledge of Jehovah, as the waters cover the sea."

FOR DISCUSSION

A. *Based on This Chapter*

1. Name the four elements that are included in the great process of transformation.
2. What is meant by the great conflagration?
3. By the glorious rejuvenation?
4. By the wonderful self-realization?
5. By the perfect harmonization?

B. *Further Discussion*

1. Does II Peter 3:10 prove that the universe will be destroyed by a U (ranium) bomb?
2. Do such passages as Romans 8:18-22 and Isaiah 11:6-9 imply that there will be plants and animals in the new world?
3. Prove that the Isaiah 11 passage has its anticipatory fulfilment in the *present* dispensation.
4. Does the *catastrophic* consummation of all things, as vividly described in II Peter 3:8-13, harmonize or clash with the idea of evolution? If a person is not sound in his doctrine of Creation, will he be sound in his doctrine of The Last Things?
5. How would you compare the universe as it existed before the fall with the universe as it is going to be after the great conflagration?

Chapter 49

The Final State of the Righteous.
What Did Jesus Say about the
Home in Glory?

Read Deuteronomy 33:27a; John 14:1-4

1. That Home Needed

In the heart of God's child there is a *longing,* yes even a *need,* for the everlasting home. As he grows older and loses or is about to lose a devout mother, trusting sister, witness-bearing father, loyal and loving wife, etc., his attention is drawn away from the earth and fixed upon heaven. If he be a minister, he may have preached about heaven a good many times, but when sorrow enters his own home and he begins to notice that the earthly tent-dwelling of one very dear to him is being rapidly dismantled, he cannot help becoming more heavenly-minded than before. What was once a sermon has become a confession of the heart. It remains a sermon, to be sure, but a better sermon than ever before.

Yes, the heavenly home is needed, for on earth nothing satisfies. There is trouble upon trouble. That, too, was the case with respect to the disciples. So on this last night before his crucifixion, being gathered with his disciples in the Upper Room, Jesus said to them (as I like to translate it):

"*Let* not y o u r *hearts* any *long*er be *tro*ubled."

The hearts of the disciples were filled with a medley of emotions. They were *sad* because of the gloomy prospect of Christ's departure; *ashamed* because of their own demonstrated selfishness and pride; *perplexed* because of the prediction that one of their own number would betray the Master, that another would deny him, and that all would be ensnared because of him; and finally, they were *wavering* in their faith, probably thinking, "How can one who is about to be betrayed be the Messiah?" Yet, at the same time, they love this Master. They hope against hope. So Jesus says to them:

"Continue to trust in God, also in me continue to trust."

2. That Home Described

Jesus continues, "In my Father's house there are many dwelling-places."

The Father's house is really a *home,* for it is a place where the children of God will enjoy *the most blessed fellowship,* as is evident from the entire context. And *that,* after all, is what changes a mere *house* into a *home.* I read somewhere that a little boy coming out of school ran into a house, and then ran out of it again very quickly. Someone who saw this asked him, "Why did you go in and then run out so quickly?" The boy replied, "I got into the wrong house. I thought it was ours. But ours is the house next door." The man then asked him, "But is not the house which you entered and which you left so quickly just as nice as your own?" "O yes, much finer," he replied. "Then why did you not stay there?" was the man's final question. The child answered, "Because mother is not there."

Accordingly, the first thing which we learn about our heavenly home is that it is the house that belongs to the Father of our Lord Jesus Christ (*"my* Father's house"); hence, surely *home* to him and therefore *home* to us. And being *the Father's* house, we may be sure that it will be *a very, very glorious place.* If even here and now those who turn from darkness to light experience "things which eye saw not, and the ear heard not, and which never entered into the heart of man" (I Corinthians 2:9), how much more applicable will that text be with respect to the home that is being prepared for us?

> "We speak of the land of the blest,
> A country so rich and so fair,
> And oft are its glories confessed,
> But what will it be to *be* there?"

Secondly, Jesus assures us that this home is *a very roomy place. Of course,* heaven is *a place.* We need not waste much space on this. Did not Jesus *ascend* to heaven? And are not Jesus, Enoch, and Elijah there *in body* as well as in soul? Exactly *where* heaven is, is of little importance. During the last fifty years our views of the extent of the universe have expanded to such an extent that there certainly can no longer be any legitimate doubt in any man's mind that in this vast domain there is plenty room for heaven.

Now note that Jesus says that in this one large house there are entire mansions or dwelling-places. In other words, heaven does not resemble a tenement-house, each family occupying one room perhaps. On the contrary, it is much more like a beautiful apartment-building, with ever so many completely furnished and spacious apartments or dwelling-units, and no crowding of any kind. "Plenty room in heaven, room for me but also room for y o u ," is the *one* idea that is conveyed here. (The idea of variety, degrees of glory, though true in itself, as we have seen earlier, is foreign to the present context.)

Thirdly, home is *the place of safety*. Outside the storm may be raging, as it actually was raging in the hearts of the disciples. Heaven is the place of perfect security.

Fourthly, home is *the place of rest*. Think of a babe at rest in its mother's arms, and then remember that though mother's arms may become tired because they are after all limited in strength, God's arms never weary. "The eternal God is thy dwelling-place, And underneath are the *everlasting* arms."

Fifthly, home is *the place of perfect understanding and love*. This will become clear under the next heading (3). Elsewhere you are often misunderstood, and your motives are misconstrued, but not at home, if your home is truly a home.

Finally, home is *the place of permanence. This* house, be it remembered, is not a mere tent, pitched now here, then there, sure to be dismantled or destroyed. The Father's house—*home,* according to the context—is the place where one dwells forever and ever, being *"at home* with the Lord."

3. That Home Prepared

"If it were not so, I would have told y o u, for I go to prepare a place for y o u. And when I go and prepare a place for y o u,

I come again and will take y o u to myself (or; to be face to face with me), in order that where I am y o u may be also."

The coming again is the counterpart of the going away, and refers therefore to the second coming. Jesus tells the disciples that by means of his humiliation (particularly, his death on the cross) and exaltation, he is preparing a place for his disciples. It is entirely possible that much more is implied in this glorious passage than we have now stated. Who will be able to say exactly in what manner Jesus is even now preparing our place in heaven? We shall probably never know the depth and meaning of this expression until with both soul and body we shall have entered upon our life in the new heaven and earth.

One point, however, is very touching. One might have expected Jesus to say, "And when I go and prepare a place for y o u, I come again and will take y o u *to that place*." But our Lord actually says something which is far more comforting, namely, "I will take y o u *to myself*." Christ's loving presence will be that which makes the Father's house a real home and a real heaven for the children of God. Wherever Jesus is, there, too, will his disciples be. They will even sit with him in his throne! Symbolical language? To be sure! All this is *only* a symbol. The reality will be even more glorious (see Revelation 3:12; 3:21; 14:1; 19:11, 14; 20:4).

4. That Home Reached

"And to the place where I am going y o u know the way," says Jesus. He means, "Y o u know *me; I* am the way." And this statement is a veiled invitation, "Come to the Father by means of this way," that is, by committing yourselves entirely to me for life and for death."

FOR DISCUSSION

A. *Based on This Chapter*

1. Show why the heavenly home is needed.
2. Describe that home.
3. What point in John 14:3 is so very touching?
4. What is "the way" to this home?
5. In which sense is John 14:4 a veiled invitation?

B. *Further Discussion*

1. Does the book of Revelation supply any additional information about our home in heaven? Where, and in general, what kind of information?

2. Just what, in that book, is the meaning of "the holy city, new Jerusalem"?

3. Does Revelation 21:16 tell us something about the shape and the size of heaven?

4. What is the meaning of Deuteronomy 32:11, 12?

5. Does that passage (cf. also Psalm 103:13, 14; Isaiah 63:9) shed any light on our future blessedness when we shall be "at home with the Lord"?

Chapter 50

Are There Any Further Questions and Warnings?

Read I John 3:1-3

With respect to *the believer's final bliss* many questions reach the minister. Some of these apply also to the intermediate state, for, as remarked earlier, it is not always possible to separate these two.

1. In the New Heaven and Earth What Will Be Our Relation to the Angels?

Answer: With respect to this question as well as to many others, we shall have to wait for the full answer until we get to the region of bliss. Very little has been revealed. It may be argued, perhaps, that basically this relation will remain what it is now. God created *the angels* to be *"ministering spirits* sent forth *to render service* in the interest of those who are to obtain salvation" (Hebrews 1:14). On the other hand, *man* was created *to exercise dominion* (Genesis 1:26). Is it possible, then, that even in the realm of glory angels will still be rendering service to us? (See, however, Question 3 under *Further Discussion* below). It can hardly be doubted that redeemed man will remain forever a *higher* creature than the angels (I Corinthians 6:3; cf. Revelation 5:11). It is also certain that even in the realm of glory the angels will learn a great deal from us (cf. Ephesians 3:10), and it is probable that we shall learn much from them and from their songs in adoration of God and the Lamb (Revelation 5:11, 12; 7:11, 12).

Between the redeemed and the angels there is ever a close relationship.

Angels Are:

*A*ttendants of Christ (II Thessalonians 1:7), *their and our* exalted Head (Ephesians 1:21, 22; Colossians 2:10).

Bringers of good tidings concerning our salvation, having seen the Lord not only in his birth but also in his resurrection and post-resurrection glory (I Timothy 3:16; cf. Luke 2:14; 24:4; Acts 1:11).

Choristers of heaven (I Corinthians 13:1; cf. Luke 15:10; Revelation 5:11, 12).

Defenders of God's children (II Thessalonians 1:7-10; cf. Psalm 91:11; Daniel 6:22; 10:10, 13, 20; Matthew 18:10; Acts 5:19; Revelation 12:7), though the latter outrank them and will judge them (I Corinthians 6:3; cf. Hebrews 1:14).

Examples in obedience (I Corinthians 11:10; cf. Matthew 6:10).

Friends of the redeemed, constantly watching them, deeply interested in their salvation, and rendering service to them in every way, also in executing the judgment of God upon the enemy (Galatians 3:19; I Corinthians 4:9; II Thessalonians 1:7; cf. Matthew 13:41; 25:31, 32; Luke 16:22; I Peter 1:12; Hebrews 1:14; Revelation 20:1-3).

"Glory to God" is ever the anthem of the angels. In the realm of perfection it will also be our anthem, and it should be that even now.

2. We Hear So Much about "Going to Heaven," but the Bible Informs Us That the Meek Will Inherit *the Earth* (Matthew 5:5). What Is Right?

Answer: In the realm of final bliss *a new heaven and a new earth,* that is, God's entire, gloriously renewed universe, will be ours to enjoy and to use for the glory of God. The conditions of holiness, joy, glory, etc., obtaining even now in heaven, will then pervade the entire redeemed universe (Revelation 21:1-3). We ourselves, both in body and soul, shall be adapted to this new universe.

3. In View of I Corinthians 15:50, Which Informs Us That *Flesh and Blood* Cannot Inherit the Kingdom of God, Is the Conclusion Warranted That the Physical Composition of the Resurrection-Body Will Be Different By and By?

Answer: As the context clearly indicates (see especially verse

50b; also verses 53 and 54), this passage does not speak about the physical composition of the resurrection-body, but informs us that our resurrection-bodies will be immortal and incorruptible, not marked by the weakness and corruptibility of our present bodies. They will resemble the transformed body of our resurrected Lord (Philippians 3:21).

4. What Is the Meaning of The Sea of Crystal?

Answer: By means of the glorious symbol of this Transparent Sea the Lord according to the context assures us that we shall see much more clearly than we do now the meaning of the ways of God's providence. God's "righteous acts" will then be "made manifest" (see Revelation 15:1-4). There is some truth in the lines:

> "Not now but in the coming years,
>   It will be in the better land,
> We'll read the meaning of our tears,
>   And there sometime we'll understand.
> We'll catch the broken threads again,
>   And finish what we here began;
> Heaven will its mysteries explain,
>   Ah then, ah then, we'll understand."
>   (Maxwell N. Cornelius)

5. When John Says, "Beloved, *Now* Are We God's Children and It Is Not Yet Made Manifest What We Shall Be," Does He Imply That When at His Second Coming Christ Is Gloriously Revealed We Shall No Longer Be Children of God but Shall Advance to a still Higher State?

Answer: And what could be "higher" than being a child of God? See I John 3:1. We are children now. We shall be children then. But the glory which these children will one day possess has not yet been publicly displayed. Not yet are we wearing the crown of victory. Not yet have we entered the new heaven and earth. Not yet do we have bodies that resemble Christ's glorious body.

6. In General, with Respect to the Believer's State of Blessedness, What Are Some of the False Ideas against Which You Would Warn?

Answer: First, I would issue a serious warning against going beyond that which Scripture has revealed, whether clearly and in so many words or by safe inference.

Secondly, I would warn against the position, apparently held by some, that the life hereafter (whether in the intermediate or in the final state) will be so altogether different that there will be no connection between it and our present state. Thus, erroneously, the preservation of personal identity is denied, whether explicitly or implicitly.

Thirdly, I would warn against any doctrine of the last things which places all the emphasis on the fact that the believer will rejoice in the absence of pain, worry, labor, sickness, etc., but forgets that it is especially the absence of *sin* (as the root of all of these) that should cause us to rejoice.

And finally, in close connection with the preceding, I would warn against all *man*-centered ideas concerning the everlasting joys of the new heaven and earth. What we should look forward to is the enjoyment of *the resplendent glory of our God.* Such passages as Psalm 73:25; Romans 11:36; I Corinthians 10:31; Revelation 7:15; 21:3; 22:3, 4 have their application here.

FOR DISCUSSION

A. *Based on This Chapter*

1. In the new heaven and earth what will be our relation to the angels?

2. Will believers inherit heaven or earth?

3. What is the meaning of The Transparent Sea?

4. Explain I John 3:2.

5. With respect to the believer's final bliss what are some of the false ideas against which we should guard ourselves?

B. *Further Discussion*

1. Does Romans 8:16, 17 shed any light on the exclamation contained in I John 3:1?

2. What exactly is the meaning of I John 3:1b?

3. Is it possible to infer from Hebrews 1:14 that once we have obtained salvation, the angels will no longer render service to us?

4. Explain I Corinthians 6:3a.

5. Explain I Peter 1:12: "which things angels desire to look into."

Index of Subjects

Index of Scripture Passages

That Appear at the Head of the Chapters

Index of Authors

---

[1] All the references are to *Gereformeerde Dogmatiek*, third edition, Vol. IV, except the one on pp. 98, 99 which is to that portion of Vol. II which I translated into English, and which was published under the title *The Doctrine of God*.